Art & craft

CHRIS HEALD

Published by Scholastic Ltd,
Villiers House,
Clarendon Avenue,
Leamington Spa,
Warwickshire CV32 5PR

1 2 3 4 5 6 7 8 9 0   6 7 8 9 0 1 2 3 4 5

Author
Chris Heald

Editor
Libby Russell

Series designer
Lynne Joesbury

Designer
Rachel Warner

Illustrations
Gaynor Berry

Cover photograph
Fiona Pragoff

Designed using Aldus Pagemaker
Printed in Great Britain by Hartnolls Ltd

British Library Cataloguing-in-Publication Data
A catalogue record for this book is available from the British Library.

ISBN 0-590-53716-4

CONTENTS

CHAPTER FIVE: PHYSICAL DEVELOPMENT

CHAPTER SIX: CREATIVE DEVELOPMENT

PHOTOCOPIABLES

INTRODUCTION

Free play is the most important type of play in early years learning and should form a large part of any good nursery provision. This does not mean leaving children alone to play while the adults do something else. Children need to be offered lots of different experiences which enable them to find out for themselves the way things work. They need to play with adults who will spend time finding out what they understand and then help them to progress. Good early years provision of any kind will encourage children to be adventurous but safe, providing an environment which will develop the learning of these future adults.

Desirable Outcomes have been produced by SCAA (Schools' Curriculum and Assessment Authority) to provide goals for learning for children by the time they enter compulsory education. They cover traditional expectations of what young children should be able to do, and the skills they should develop. Within a normal range of abilities, some children will be able to do all that is expected of them, most will be able to do some things and not others, while some children will achieve hardly any of these outcomes before they are five years of age.

Setting up the environment

The environment for art and craft should include boards at the children's height for them to display their own work, spacious surfaces for spreading materials around and trying lots of tools, as much wipe-clean floor as possible and plenty of storage for materials. The following should be accessible to the children when they want to use them: paper, paint of different kinds, adhesives, collage materials, recycled materials, brushes and rollers, sticks, pencils, crayons, felt-tipped pens, biros, Plasticine, playdough and so on. Trolleys which hold up to 18 plastic trays are ideal for storing art and craft materials and these are available from most educational suppliers.

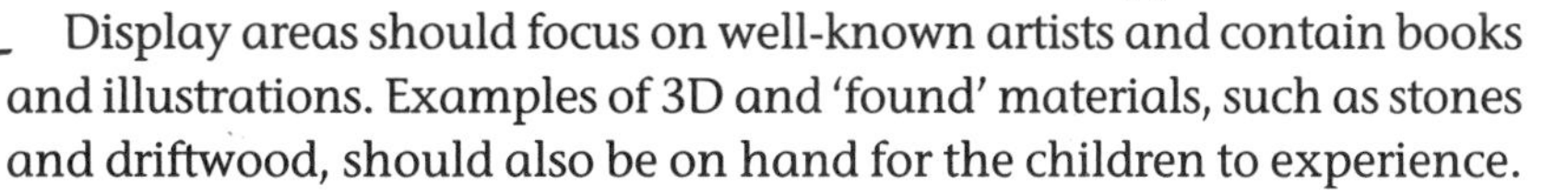

Display areas should focus on well-known artists and contain books and illustrations. Examples of 3D and 'found' materials, such as stones and driftwood, should also be on hand for the children to experience.

Whenever children are undertaking craft or cookery activities, ensure that they cover their clothing with a protective apron. Most of the activities in this book will require the children to wear aprons and this will not be stated every time in the individual instructions.

Observation and assessment

In order to observe and assess, it is first necessary to understand what you can expect of the children and this is what the Desirable Outcomes are designed to tell us. Working with the children, and offering activities which are aimed at developing certain aspects of the Desirable Outcomes, will enable you to keep records of their work during and after the activity. At the end of a session you should have a good idea of what the children can and cannot do, and what they need to do next to develop their skills. This information can be kept to form part of the child's Record of Achievement for their early years.

Using adult helpers

Adults working with young children provide a strong motivating force both for learning and behaviour. You can offer the children experiences in which they take the lead and you act as an enabler, making suggestions which may or may not be accepted and used. A very important tool which can be used is the questioning technique. Asking open-ended questions which do not have a simple 'yes' or 'no' answer, invites the children to tell you at length about their experience. For example 'Did you like that?' is a question to which the only answer is 'yes' or 'no', while 'What are you doing?' needs an explanation from the child and can result in a conversation. There is also a need for you to tell the children facts which will enhance their learning in the course of the conversation.

Types of art activities

Drawing and painting: For a young child, drawing and painting is a way of communicating without words in order to explore and express experiences. Adults who work with young children should be aware that they need as many first-hand art experiences as possible in order to stimulate their creative thought. Children also need time to investigate materials and their properties thoroughly if they are to learn how to use them properly and with control. In this way the children will develop sensitivity in responding to the world around them and have improved self-images of themselves as creative people.

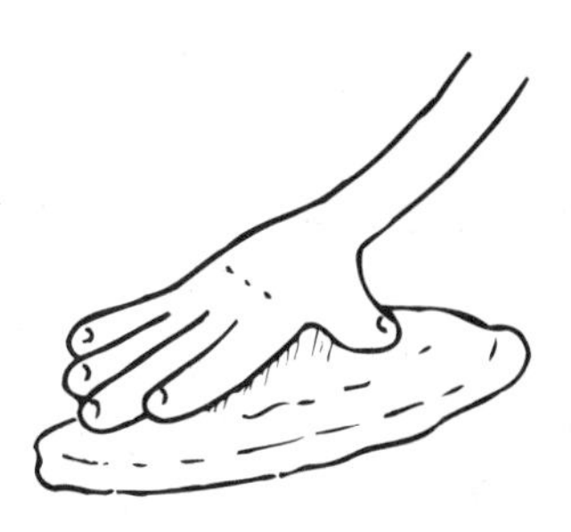

Manipulative 3D materials: Children love to use their hands and explore what they can do with a material, sometimes testing it to destruction. Play with clay and dough enables them to experiment in a very physical way, pummelling, chopping, pinching, poking and so on. As well as being a learning experience, 3D materials can be therapeutic: children can sometimes sit smoothing or kneading clay, completely engrossed and obviously deriving great pleasure and relaxation from what they are doing. Time to explore is very important to early years children, and they will not benefit from a hurried activity.

Craft/design in the wider world: Examples of fabric and ceramics, posters, wallpaper and carpets can all be used with young children to develop particular skills and techniques. Activities using simple forms of batik, looking at Islamic patterns on carpets or Art Nouveau decoration can provide interesting experiences for young children. Craft ideas in this book have concentrated on a theme of puppets, since this is appropriate for children and introduces the concept of designing an object for a purpose, and also following a pattern to produce similar but individual products.

Printing: There are many methods and tools which can be used for printing, starting with hand printing with a variety of types of paint, developing into printing with solid and natural objects, progressing to the use of pliable materials such as string, spaghetti and Plasticine. Children can make their own 'something' which can be used to print with, using adhesive, corrugated card or soap. Printing can be random or regular, a single colour, an alternating colour or a wild mixture of colours. It is sometimes a good thing to restrict the children's choice of colours or materials so that they can experience an effect which they may be too young to discover and use for themselves, such as using pastel colours or monochrome.

Links with home

Home is a very important place for young children, and the more links which can be created, the better they will settle. Home visits are an excellent idea if they can be arranged and someone can be freed to do it. Parents should be invited to stay with their children when they first start attending, to help the child feel at home.

Invite parents to come and work with the children. This is a common practice in playgroups and a growing one in nurseries of all kinds. Recent developments with National Vocational Qualifications (known as NVQs) mean that volunteering parents can undergo training and become qualified.

Good communication between home and yourself is very important. Have some leaflets printed which tell new parents all about the service you offer. Send a newsletter home with the children every now and then, to tell parents what you have been doing. Put a different notice up every week, telling parents one of the things you have been doing this week.

Items brought from home by the children can give them that extra boost in their confidence, encouraging and enabling them to talk to other children.

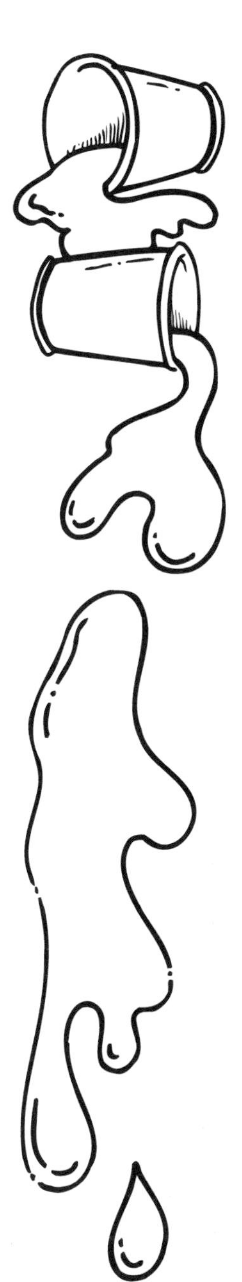

Health and safety

The health and safety issues to consider with art and craft centre mostly on hygiene and safe storage. The area where the children play must be kept clean, and toilet facilities must be available on demand. Any tools used will need to be washed and sterilised at intervals to make sure that germs are not passed from child to child.

When young children need a piece of paper they tend to just pull at the nearest piece, therefore, overfilled cupboards or paper heaped in piles on surfaces can be hazardous due to their instability.

Always use non-poisonous paints and adhesives. Try to find out about children with allergies to certain colourings and make sure they are not exposed to them when finger-painting or playing in water or sand. Tools which are pointed or sharp should only be used when adult supervision is available and children should be taught to use scissors responsibly.

Throughout the book, reference to safety issues are highlighted through the use of the word CARE!

How to use this book

All the activities in this book have been written with the Desirable Outcomes in mind. For each of the six areas you will find eight activities which are intended to develop a child's skill mainly in that area. The topic web on page 10 shows you which activities are intended to develop which areas. However, many of the activities relate to more than one Desirable Outcome, and when you offer them to your children, you may find that you are working with language and mathematical concepts, developing social and personal skills, and creative skills all at the same time. This integrated approach is an excellent way for young children to learn.

Use this book as you would use a recipe book, adding your own personal touches and ideas to the outline of the activities. Do not expect very young children to be interested in the end product of every activity. They enjoy experimenting with tools, materials and techniques, and are learning when they can actively cut, stick, paint, poke with sticks, dab with sponges and so on. Listen to the children and let them take you where they want to go, to explore areas which interest them, since this is the best way to produce children who are highly motivated to learn.

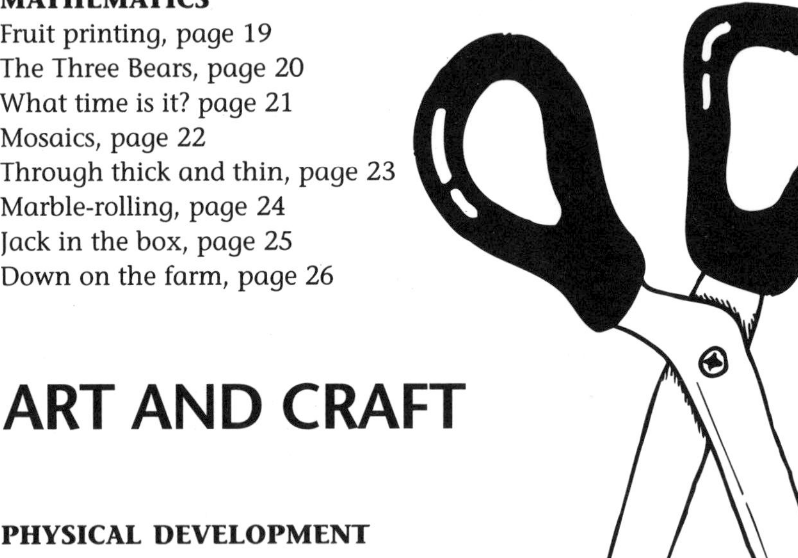

ART AND CRAFT

LANGUAGE AND LITERACY

Art and craft materials provide ideal opportunities for nursery children to develop their language skills. The ability to listen attentively and speak clearly is essential for their future education. In this chapter you will find activities to enable children to make puppets, talk about their experiences and write their names.

SPAGHETTI SNAKES

Learning objective
To talk about an experience.

Group size
Four children.

What you need

A large packet of dry spaghetti (this would be enough for several groups), washing-up liquid, pearlised paint, dark coloured paper, a small baby-bath or similar container, a drying rack of some kind.

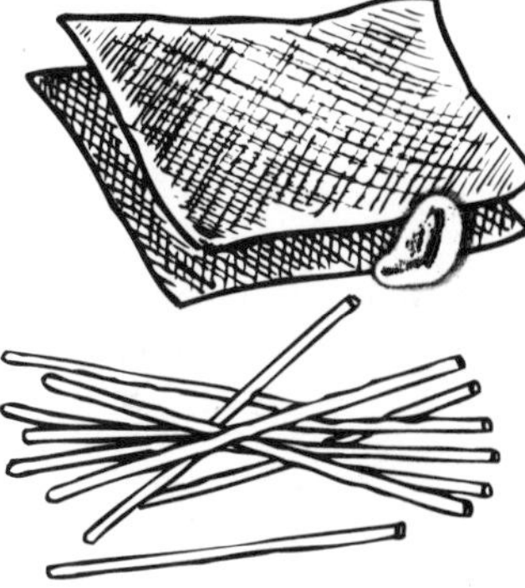

Setting up

Cook the spaghetti and allow it to go cold. This can be done with the children, but is best done the day before you intend doing the rest of the activity. Provide a piece of dark coloured paper for each child.

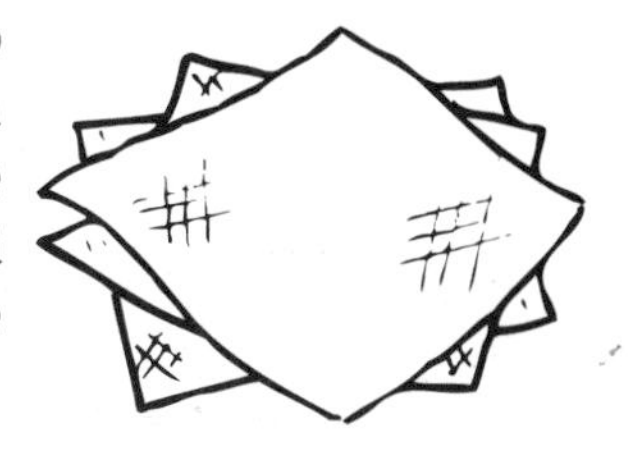

What to do

Put some of the spaghetti in the baby bath and invite the children to feel it. Add enough washing-up liquid to make the spaghetti feel slippery and slimy (be aware of children with allergies). Let the group spend some time running it through their fingers. Ask the children about this 'tactile' experience, do not rush them. When you feel the children are ready, add some pearlised paint to the spaghetti and invite the children to lift some of the coloured spaghetti onto the dark paper and make a print.

Questions to ask

How does the spaghetti feel now? What does it remind you of? What do you think would happen if we put sand into it? Would it feel the same? Why? Is it easy to get hold of one strand of spaghetti? Why?

For younger children

Younger children enjoy just feeling the spaghetti and the washing-up liquid. They tend to find it difficult to lift the spaghetti up, so provide support to help them achieve this.

For older children

Older children could make a more complex print with several small amounts of spaghetti in different colours. They could then write about how it felt.

Follow-up activities

- Use a pasta-machine to squeeze out raw pasta dough into pasta shapes.
- Cook the shapes and then use them as in the main activity.
- Make a pasta collage using the different shapes.
- Use vegetable dyes to colour macaroni and when it is dry, make bracelets and necklaces by threading the macaroni onto pieces of string.

RUB A DUB DUB

Learning objective
To develop early writing skills by taking rubbings.

Group size
Four children.

What you need

Several brass embossed plates of the kind to be found in jumble or car-boot sales, paper, wax crayons, Blu-Tack, Sellotape.

Setting up

Take any paper off the wax crayons so that they can be used sideways. Anchor the brass plates to the surface by placing Blu-Tack underneath them and pressing down firmly.

What to do

Show the children how to fix a piece of paper to the brass plate with Sellotape so that it will not move. Demonstrate how to use the side of the crayons to give a pale background to make the embossed patterns stand out. Invite the children to choose a plate and use a variety of coloured crayons to make a picture. Encourage them to compare their finished rubbings with the original plate.

Questions to ask

Which plate did you choose? What pattern have you got on your plate? How are you going to make your picture? Which colours are you going to use? Why? How is your rubbing different from the pattern on the plate?

For younger children

Give younger children plenty of experience with the concept of rubbing, using commercially-produced embossed plastic figures stuck firmly to a card base as a starting point. They may also find it easier to use the ends of crayons at first, rather than the sides.

For older children

Older children could combine parts of different rubbings to make a new picture. They could also cut out their rubbings and make a collage-style picture using the separate pieces.

Follow-up activities
- Collect objects, such as coins, which can be fastened with Blu-Tack to a baseboard and used to take rubbings.
- Collage pictures made out of materials like corrugated card, could be used to take rubbings.
- Go outside and take rubbings of tree trunks. Discover how different varieties of trees make different bark patterns.

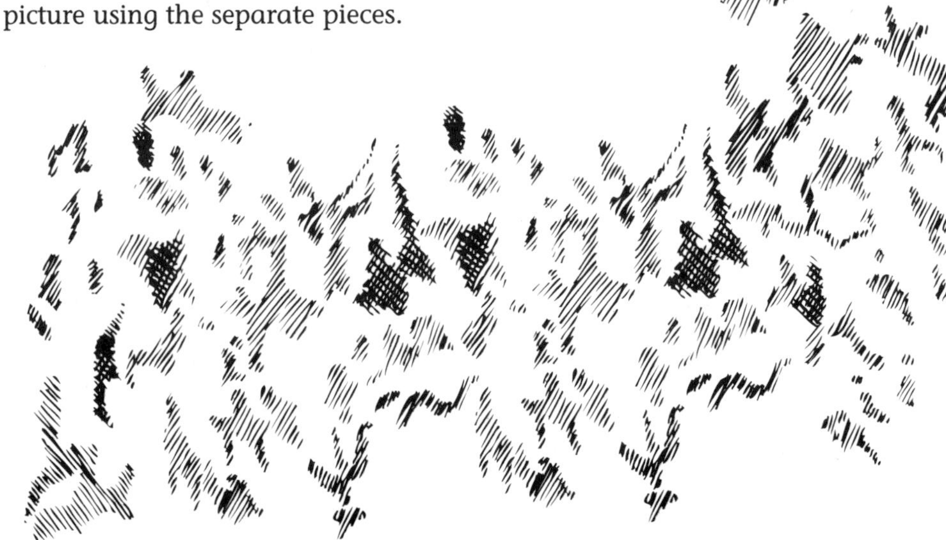

PAPER-BAG PUPPETS

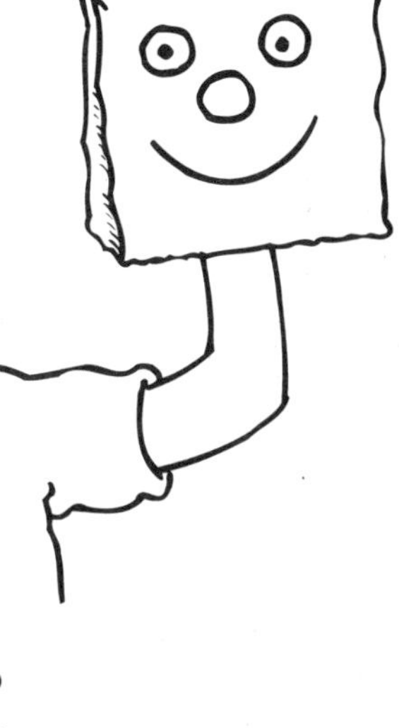

Learning objective
To enable the children to speak in character and to take part in role-play with confidence.

Group size
Six children.

What you need

Small paper bags – big enough for a child's hand, thick and thin felt-tipped pens, a storybook with simple repeating dialogue, such as *The Gingerbread Boy* or *Chicken Licken* (Traditional).

Setting up

Read the story with the children, talking about the characters and how they speak to each other.

What to do

Show the children how a paper bag will fit over their hand and when a face is drawn on, it turns into a puppet. Invite the children to make a puppet of one of the characters in the story, using the felt-tipped pens. When they have made one puppet, and are using it on one hand, ask if they would like to make another for the other hand, so that the puppets can talk to each other. Then ask the children to tell you what each puppet is saying to the other, starting off with the dialogue from the story you have read.

Questions to ask

Which puppet have you made? How did you make it? What colours have you used? What can your puppet do? What can your puppet say? Who to? What did this one say in the story? What did the other one say?

For younger children

Younger children may find it easier to make one puppet and then to make it talk to another child's puppet or themselves.

For older children

Older children could make up a complete play of the story, using a puppet for each character and record it on tape, or write it down. Help them to design and make a puppet-theatre and then to perform their play for parents and friends.

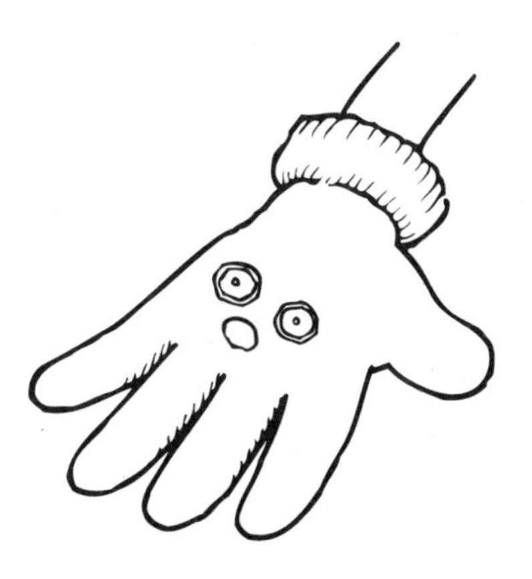

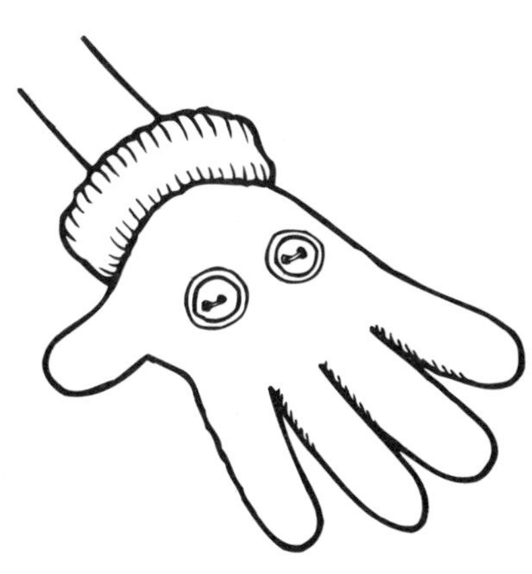

Follow-up activities

- Draw faces on paper plates, add two dangling legs made of string, wool or zigzag-folded paper to each plate, using a stapler. Thread string through a hole in the top of the plate and make the puppets dance.
- Find some old socks or gloves and glue some eyes onto them.
- Stuff old tights with cut up pieces of material to make snake or worm puppets. Add felt spots for decoration and eyes, then use a strip of red felt for a tongue. Attach a piece of string and drag the wriggling puppet across the floor.

GLITTER WRITING

Learning objective
To recognise, read and write their own names with appropriate use of upper and lower case letters.

Group size
Six children.

What you need
Adhesive pens, different colours of glitter, sheets of stiff paper or card, metallic foil, tinsel, a hole-punch, metallic Christmas parcel-wrapping ribbon, newspaper, pencils, scissors.

Setting up
Cut your paper or card into the shape of large labels (see illustration). Encourage the children to punch a hole in one end.

What to do
Ask the children to write their first names across their luggage label using a pencil. For those children who are still unsure how to write their name, you could write it for them on a piece of paper, show it to them and ask them to trace the letters in the air. Then put your paper away and ask the children to remember how their name is written by writing it on the label. Allow another peep if they have forgotten parts of their name, but they should not be encouraged to copy each letter, since the idea is to develop their memory so that they can remember the shape of their name.

Once the names have been written, encourage the children to use the adhesive pen to cover the letters with glue and finally sprinkle their choice of glitter over the writing so that it looks as if it has been iced onto the paper with glitter icing. Cut out the shapes of birthday/ Christmas presents and attach the labels to them. Put them on the wall to display.

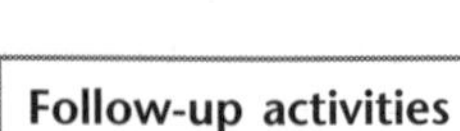

Questions to ask
What letters can you see in your name? What sound does that letter make? Where can you see your name? Whose name is this? What else can you write? What colours are you going to put on your name?

For younger children
Younger children will be able to do this activity using emergent writing. This is where they know some letters of their name but do not know them all, use the same letter repeatedly, or use letters and numbers they know which may or may not be in their name. Accept this early writing with enthusiasm!

For older children
Older children may be able to write their second name as well as their first. They may also wish to write Christmas greetings and decorate them as above.

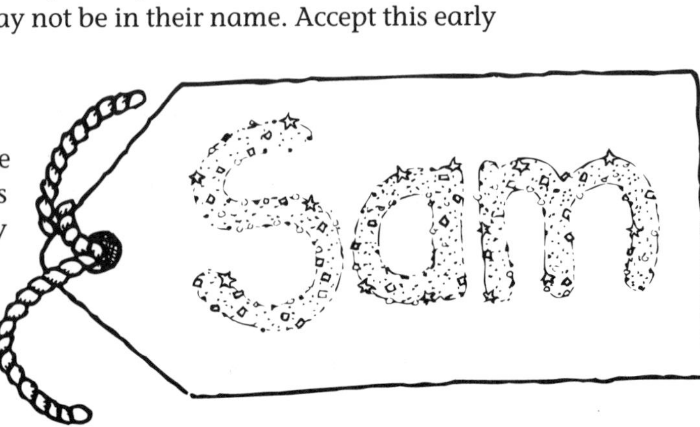

Follow-up activities
- Make patterns in the same way on crowns or costumes to look like jewels or embroidery.
- Pipe some PVA adhesive in a pattern onto a piece of rigid card. Use this as a printing block when it is fully dry. Use a plastic syringe to pipe the adhesive (this is an economical alternative to using adhesive-spreaders, and cheaper than buying pens).

NURSERY RHYMES

Learning objective
To develop understanding of how books are organised, and to know that words and pictures carry meaning.

Group size
Six children.

What you need

A wide choice of writing/drawing tools – pastels, biros, roller ball-type ink pens, felt-tipped pens, wax crayons, A4 sheets of paper, A4 plastic pockets and a ring-binder to put them in, a book of nursery rhymes such as Quentin Blake's *Nursery Rhyme Book* (Red Fox).

Setting up

Put all the writing/drawing tools where the children can reach them easily and choose freely.

What to do

Read some of the nursery rhymes in the book with your group. Talk about the pictures, and how they illustrate the words of the rhymes. Ask the children if they know any nursery rhymes. Listen to their comments, then ask them if they would like to make a book with all their nursery rhymes in. Let each child decide which nursery rhyme they are going to illustrate.

Invite the children to choose the tools they want to use, and to write their rhyme if they wish. You may not be able to read what they write, but it is important to accept the marks they make as writing, so that they view themselves as writers from the start of their writing experience. Ask the children to read what they have written back to you, or if they have just drawn pictures, to describe these to you. Show the children how to slide their rhymes into the plastic pockets and put them into the ring-binder. Put the book into the book-corner for all to see.

Questions to ask

Which nursery rhyme are you going to draw a picture of? Why did you choose that one? Why did you choose that to write/draw with? What have you drawn/written? What could you do next?

For younger children

Younger children can be invited to do this activity, but should not be expected to produce recognisable pictures or legible writing. Praise their work and put it in the book in the same way as above, so that they too can be proud of their work.

For older children

Older children could number the pages of the book correctly, make a contents list at the front and an index of first lines at the back. They could then write the names of the authors on the front of the book.

Follow-up activities

- Put a tape of well-known nursery rhymes in a corner where the children can choose to go and switch it on to listen. Several headphones and a junction-box can be useful here if noise is a problem.
- Try to provide props for nursery rhyme play in the role-play corner. Have a cushion called Humpty Dumpty, collect some Christmas silver bells and some seaside cockleshells for 'Mary, Mary', and find a toy lamb.
- Invite the children to say their favourite rhymes during carpet time.

WHAT DO YOU LIKE?

Learning objective
To recognise and write familiar words, and to develop cutting skills.

Group size
Eight children.

What you need
Toy catalogues, magazines, small scissors with rounded ends, adhesive sticks, pencils, a sheet of paper or a book of blank paper for each child, a pad of paper, a black felt-tipped pen.

Setting up
Ensure that the scissors you are expecting the children to use do cut paper. Write the words 'I like' on the pad, making sure that it can be covered by another page if needed.

What to do
Sit with the children and ask them about the things they like. Look at the two words 'I like' and talk about their shape and what they mean. Invite the children to find pictures of things they like in the magazines, cut around them and stick them on their paper. Encourage each child to write 'I like cars/dolls' and so on. If some children feel they cannot write 'I' or 'like', let them have a quick look at what you have written, but then cover it up and ask them to try to remember and write it.

This approach helps children to develop a sense of whether a word 'looks right' while giving them the confidence to write creatively.

Questions to ask
Which of these do you like best? Why? What are you going to cut out? What do you use that for? How will you stick it onto your paper? What are you going to write? Where do you start writing? What else could you write?

For younger children
Younger children find cutting around objects difficult and need to be taught how to move the paper with their non-cutting hand, so that they are not trying to cut sideways, but always straight up. Cutting and sticking will be an activity in itself, but encourage the children to make marks on their paper. Accept what they decide to do, even if it appears to be scribble.

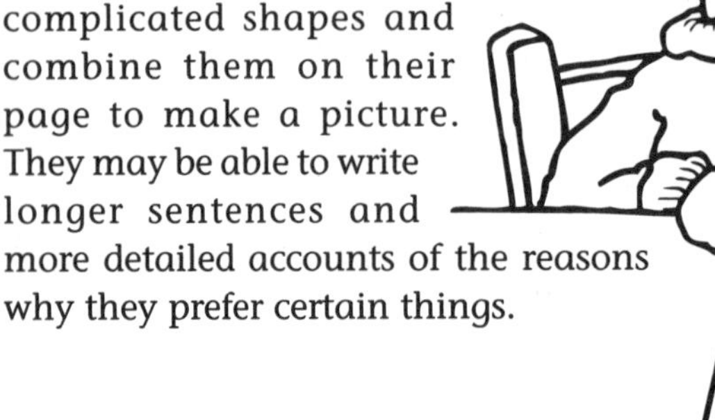

For older children
Older and more able children could cut out more complicated shapes and combine them on their page to make a picture. They may be able to write longer sentences and more detailed accounts of the reasons why they prefer certain things.

Follow-up activities
- Select pictures and combine them to cover boxes and exercise books in the 'découpage' technique used on Victorian screens. Cover with a glaze made from PVA adhesive and water.
- To obtain a 3D effect, using self-adhesive pads behind cut-out pictures to make them stand out from the background.

BEAUTIFUL BUTTERFLIES

Learning objective
To listen and respond to a story in a group.

Group size
Six children.

What you need

A copy of *The Very Hungry Caterpillar* by Eric Carle (Hamish Hamilton), sheets of acetate (used for overhead projectors), brightly coloured Cromar paint (Berol) in squeezable bottles – this paint does not mix, its colours remain separate when swirled together, it is also translucent.

Setting up

Help the children to fold their acetate sheet in half, squeeze it and open it out again.

What to do

Read the story of *The Very Hungry Caterpillar* with the children. Encourage them to join in with the finishing line 'and he was *still* hungry'. Talk about the different food he ate, and how he felt. Look at the picture of the butterfly and ask if the children would like to make some butterfly pictures to put on the window.

Invite them to squeeze blobs of Cromar onto the lower side of their acetate sheet, fold the top sheet over and then rub the blobs with their fingers. The children will enjoy seeing the colours move around under pressure from their hands. Talk about what they see. When they are ready, they can open their sheet to see their butterfly picture. If they want to, let them refold it and spread out the paint further. The butterflies take a day or so to dry, and can then be hung or stuck to the windows, where the light will shine through them like a stained-glass window.

Questions to ask

What did the caterpillar eat on Saturday? What do caterpillars usually eat? How did it make him feel? What happened to the caterpillar? Where would you go if you had beautiful butterfly wings? Which colours are you going to use for your butterfly? Why?

For younger children

Younger children may find acetate too difficult to fold, so let them use white or coloured paper instead.

For older children

In addition to experimenting with folding their acetate in different ways for different effects, older children could investigate other ways of making symmetrical pictures, for example, they could cut magazine pictures in half, and then draw the missing half in crayon or pencil.

Follow-up activities

- Using a piece of A5 coloured paper cut out pieces of any shape from it. Stick the remaining pattern and the cut-out pieces onto a piece of white paper to make a positive/negative pattern (see illustration).
- Try some wax crayon symmetry. Fold a piece of A4 paper in half, and draw a picture on one half using wax crayon. Colour the picture very thickly. An adult can then iron the folded paper so that the image appears upside-down on the other half of the sheet.

PATTERNS IN THE SAND

Learning objective
To recognise letters of the alphabet by shape and sound, and to write them.

Group size
Ten children.

What you need

An easel with a piece of paper clipped to it with a bulldog clip, a thick black marker, dry silver sand in shallow trays – one for each child, coloured sand (available from educational suppliers), or powder paint and silver sand, tubs to hold the sand, PVA adhesive and spreaders or solid rub-on adhesive, black or coloured paper.

Setting up

To make a suitable coloured sand, mix dry silver sand with 25% powder paint, putting a single colour in each tub. Decide on the letter you are going to work with. In general, it is best to group letters in 'families' of similar shapes and introduce them together. The usual groups are: aocdge / ilj / pb/ hnmr/ tf/ vwy/ qu /sz /kx.

What to do

Gather the children around you and write your chosen letter on the easel, pointing out to them where you start the letter, the direction you move the marker, and where you finish. Talk about the sound each letter makes. Encourage them to write the letter in the air, copying your movements. Give each child a sand tray with a thin layer of dry silver sand in the bottom, and encourage them to draw the letter in the sand, shaking the tray to clear it – they can repeat it as many times as they wish. Then ask the children to make a letter using coloured paper and adhesive, and sprinkling coloured sand along the path of the glue. When dry, encourage them to close their eyes and run their fingertips over the shape of the letters they have made.

Questions to ask

What sound does this letter make? Which way are you going to make this line go? What colours are you going to use? What does the sand feel like? What else could you do?

Follow-up activities
- Make some letter-shapes using velvet or textured paper, stick them on some card and run your fingers over them during play.
- Paint a picture with adhesive and then sprinkle different colours of sand on top.
- Try sticking other materials to make letter-shapes, such as sawdust, glitter, wood shavings, tissue-paper, seeds and so on.

For younger children

Younger children may not be ready to copy letter shapes, but will be able to make patterns with an adhesive-spreader and sprinkle sand over them. This is essential early experience which will prepare the children for making letter-shapes later.

For older children

Older children might like to write their names using adhesive and sprinkle them with sand. They might also be able to write words using adhesive describing the feel of the sand, to make a 'tactile poem'.

Art and craft activities can be mathematical! Explore the properties of geometric shapes by printing with them or by making junk models and develop spatial awareness while painting pictures.

FRUIT PRINTING

Learning objective
To match colours of fruit to colours of paint.

Group size
Six to eight children.

What you need

Fruit of all different shapes, ready-mixed paint of different colours including those usually associated with the fruit you have available, powder paint, enough saucers or trays for each colour, rounded knives suitable for child use, large sheets of paper.

Setting up

Encourage the children to pour a single colour of paint into each of the trays or saucers.

What to do

Ask the children if they can cut the fruit in half using the knives you have provided (help children with any difficult fruit, such as grapefruit). Cut the fruit in several different directions and look at the shapes made – cut a pear in half horizontally and there are circles; cut an apple in half horizontally and you will find a star in the middle. Then demonstrate how the pieces can be dipped into the paint and used to make patterns. Talk about the colours of the fruit and ask the children if they can make their prints the same colour as their fruit. They can then experiment with different colours and add the powder paint to change the shades of colour. CARE! Make sure, throughout this activity, that the children are not tempted to eat the fruit.

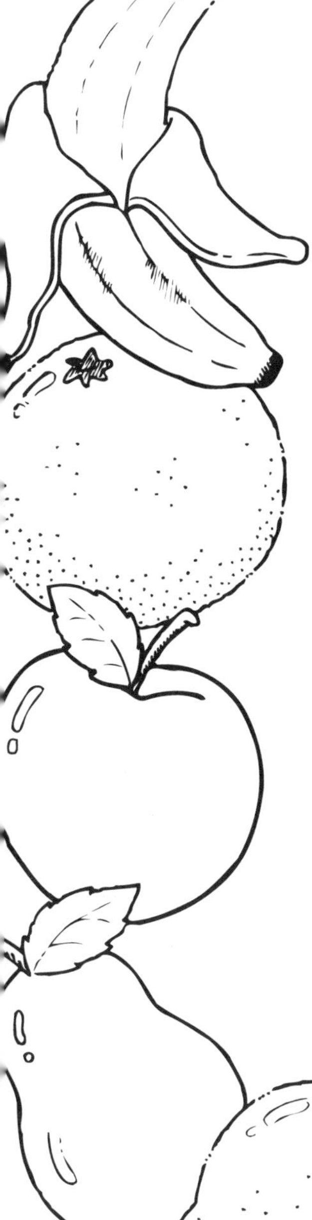

Questions to ask

What shape does that piece make? What pattern are you going to make now? Are you going to print in a line or all over the page? Why? How could you make this paint the same colour as your apple? What is your favourite fruit? Where do you get it from?

For younger children

Help younger children to cut their fruit up. Encourage them to experiment freely with the fruit printing at first, rather than matching colours correctly at first. This can be discussed while talking about their printing picture.

For older children

Older children could be asked to create a picture of fruit trees or a fruit bowl using their fruit prints. They could cut out a bowl using gummed paper, stick it onto their large sheet of paper and then print the fruit so that it 'fills' the bowl.

Follow-up activities

- Taste some of the fruit you have been using (obviously not the ones used for printing). Use a blindfold or shut your eyes. Can you tell what colour it is by the taste? (Be sensitive to dislikes and allergies.)
- Try printing with vegetables: onions, aubergines, leeks, courgettes, carrots, and mushrooms are all suitable.
- In Autumn, try printing with leaves and nuts in autumnal colours on dark coloured paper.

THE THREE BEARS

Learning objective
To work with comparative size and ordering for size.

Group size
Four children.

What you need

Three toy teddy bears, one large, one medium-sized and one small, at least one item of clothing for each bear, a set of oil-pastels, paper.

Setting up

Cut the paper into three different sizes to match the sizes of the teddy bears; make enough sets for each child.

What to do

Tell the story of *Goldilocks and The Three Bears* to your group without reading from a book, using the soft toys to illustrate. A child could play Goldilocks. Talk about your three bears. Ask the children if they could choose an item of clothing and put it on the right bear. Then ask the children to look at the pieces of paper you have cut. Talk about which bear would have which piece. Ask the children if they would like to make a set of chairs, or porridge bowls or beds for the three bears, using the different sizes of paper, and putting each of their pictures next to the bear they have drawn it for. Show the children how they can deliberately smudge and blend the colours of the oil pastels to make a more interesting effect. Demonstrate how the sides as well as the ends of the pastels can be used. Encourage the children to do their pictures to their own taste.

Questions to ask

Does this belong to Daddy Bear, Mummy Bear or Baby Bear? How can you tell? Who is the biggest? Smallest? Medium-sized? What would you do if you were in the three bears' house?

For younger children

Tell younger children the story and give them the three sizes of paper, but then let them experiment with making marks of all kinds with the pastels.

For older children

Older children could work with much more detail and draw other objects besides the ones mentioned in the story – shoes, hats, bicycles, handkerchiefs and so on.

Follow-up activities
- Cut out objects from magazines and make sets of small, medium and large goods.
- Use photocopiable page 64 to make finger-puppets of the three bears.
- Make a puppet show of the three bears using the finger-puppets.

WHAT TIME IS IT?

Learning objective
To begin to understand the times of the day and their order.

Group size
Four children.

What you need

The song 'Lazy Mary' on a tape called *Story Chest Songs* (Thomas Nelson & Sons), paper plates, coloured Plasticine, PVA adhesive.

Setting up

Soften the Plasticine by leaving it on a radiator.

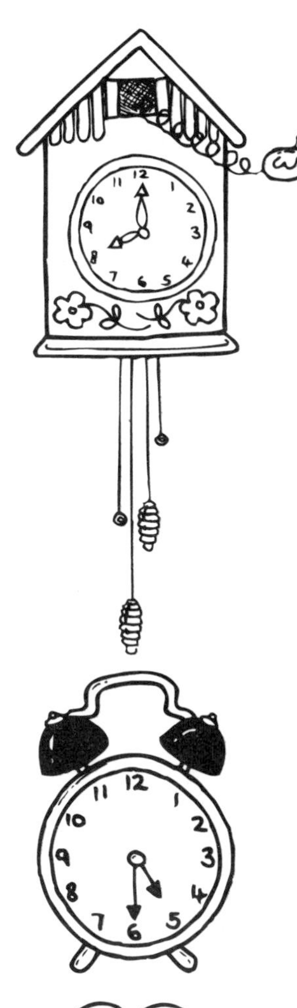

What to do

Sing the song 'Lazy Mary' to the tune of 'Here we go round the Mulberry Bush'.
Lazy Mary's Mummy starts by singing:

Lazy Mary will you get up, will you get up, will you get up,
Lazy Mary, will you get up, will you get up today?
Lazy Mary answers:
What will you give me if I get up, if I get up, if I get up,
What will you give me if I get up, if I get up today?
(These remain the same throughout the song.)
The (spoken) answer is:
1. *A nice egg for your breakfast.*
2. *A nice pie for your dinner.*
3. *Some nice salad for your tea.*
4. *A glass of cold water all over you if you don't get up NOW!*

Three times Lazy Mary replies:
No mother I won't get up, I won't get up, I won't get up,
No mother I won't get up, I won't get up today.
But the last time, she says that she will get up!

As you come to each spoken part, ask the children what time it is if Mary is having ... an egg and so on. Then encourage the children to model their favourite food for breakfast, dinner and tea. Tell them to stick the Plasticine food onto the plates with adhesive. Then paint over the food with the adhesive to give it a glazed look.

Questions to ask

What time do you have your breakfast, dinner and tea? What do you like to eat? What don't you like? Why? Who makes your meals? Where do you eat them? Who eats it with you?

For younger children

Ask younger children to make just one plate of food, choosing whatever they like to eat best.

For older children

Older children could make more models of their favourite food in Mod Roc or Newclay. These could then be used for role-play with the children acting out meal times.

Follow-up activities
- Cut out pictures of food from magazines and paste them onto plates to make up a favourite menu.
- Talk about other events which happen at specific times of the day. When do you arrive and leave? When do you have a story?
- Make a diary so that everyone knows when they are due to do certain things.

MOSAICS

Learning objective
To recognise and re-create patterns by creating a picture using geometric shapes.

Group size
Six children.

What you need
Photocopiable page 59, felt-tipped pens in a large assortment of colours, flat geometrical mosaic shapes made of wood or plastic such as Logic blocks (Invicta), large pictures of the patterns found in Islamic art or used in Rangoli patterns.

Setting up
Spread out the shapes on the table top. Make sure you have a copy of sheet 59 for each child with a few spares. Colour in some sheets to pick out some examples of patterns to show the group.

What to do
Start by looking at the pictures of the intricate patterns found in Islamic art. Point out the geometric shapes which make up the pattern. Then make some simple patterns using the mosaic shapes with the children. Encourage them to make patterns of their own. Hand out the sheet to each child and point out the shapes on it. Show the group the examples of patterns which you have already made. Ask them if they can see a pattern and colour it in. Accept what the children produce, and talk about the patterns they have seen, comparing them with each other.

Questions to ask
What pattern have you made? What shapes have you coloured? Which colours have you used? What does your pattern look like?

For younger children
You can help younger children to understand the concept of pattern by making cards on which you have drawn outlines of patterns. The children can then put the mosaic pieces on top of the cards as a matching activity.

For older children
Older children could make their own pattern sheet by using paper with 2.5cm squares printed on it and using a ruler to create diagonal lines where wanted. Again, an example would help them to understand.

Follow-up activities
- Print with solid geometrical shapes on black paper using fluorescent paints.
- Cut up colourful pages of magazines into squares, triangles and rectangles and let the children glue a pattern onto black paper.
- Try making a mosaic of natural objects.

THROUGH THICK AND THIN

Learning objective
Experimenting with brushes of different thicknesses.

Group size
Eight children.

What you need
Paintbrushes of as many different thicknesses as possible from very thin to 15cm decorator's brushes, a variety of colours of paint, including pastel colours, trays or saucers to hold paint, long pieces of paper such as lining paper, sheets of paper.

Setting up
Cover the area of the floor where the children will be working. Make sure that the paintbrushes will fit into the trays or saucers of paint.

What to do
Invite the children to paint on the long pieces of paper, using their choice of paint and paintbrush. While they are playing, point out the differences in thickness between the various brushes they choose. Encourage the children to paint long lines with their brushes, and to wash their brush before painting in a different colour. Ask them to paint a wash on the sheets of paper with a thick brush and paint patterns with a thin brush in another colour on top once it has dried.

Questions to ask
Which brush covers the most paper? Why? Which brush did you find easiest to use? Why? Which line is thin? Which line is thick? What are you going to paint now? What could you do to make this line thicker?

For younger children
It is important to give young children plenty of time to experiment and discover what they can do with brushes and paint.

For older children
Older children could spend some time discussing the uses of the different brushes. They could plan a painting which would make use of brushes of all thicknesses for the tasks best suited to them, for example, thick brushes to paint large areas, thin brushes for fine detail. They could look at a famous painting such as Van Gogh's 'Sunflowers' and decide which brushes would be needed for each part of the painting.

Follow-up activities
- Try using thick and thin rollers, thick and thin sponges and thick and thin sticks with paint.
- Sort sets of thick and thin objects. Provide a wide range of geometrical sorting shapes.
- Use pastry or play dough and roll it into thick or thin sheets, then cut out shapes with biscuit cutters.

MARBLE-ROLLING

Learning objective
To explore some of the properties of spheres, and to use mathematical language to describe a shape.

Group size
Six children.

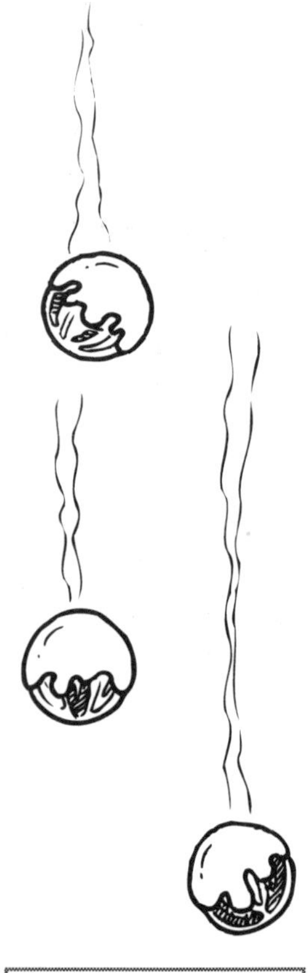

What you need
Six marbles, some trays with high sides on which marbles can roll from side to side, pearlised paint, coloured or white paper.

Setting up
Put paper in the bottom of some trays. Keep one tray empty.

CARE! This activity should be constantly supervised with younger children, as marbles could be dangerous if placed in mouths.

What to do
Ask the children to pour their choice of paint into a tray. Encourage them to handle the marbles and talk about their shape – what will they do because they are that shape? Show the children how to roll the marbles around inside the empty tray before encouraging them to drop the marbles into the tray with their chosen colour of paint, and then roll the coated marbles back and forth across a piece of paper in the other trays. Encourage them to look at their patterns and decide if they want to add more to them.

Questions to ask
What colours are you going to use? What can you make the marble do? How do you make it move? What shape does it make? Why? What would happen if you dropped the marbles onto the paper? What else could you dip in paint and roll?

For younger children
Some younger children may become frustrated if they cannot control the marble in the tray as they wish. Help them to understand that it does not matter where the marble rolls and emphasis the fun of its uncontrollability.

For older children
Older children could experiment with different shapes of tray such as trays with rectangular surfaces and circular surfaces, and compare the various patterns produced.

Follow-up activities
- Try printing by dipping balls of various sizes into paint. What shape do you get?
- Blow up round balloons, cover them with papier mâché and paint them. How can you keep them still?
- Make some biscuit dough and roll it into balls before cooking. What shape is it after it has been cooked?

JACK IN THE BOX

Learning objective
To use mathematical language to describe shape while making a puppet using geometric shapes.

Group size
Four children.

What you need

Photocopiable page 60, solid adhesive sticks, felt-tipped pens, wooden lolly sticks, card, scissors, sticky-backed plastic, split pins.

Setting up

Make an example of the finished pop-up to show the children so that they can see what the finished version will be like (see illustration). Stick all the pieces together and attach the arms with some split pins. Make sure you have a copy of photocopiable page 60 for each child and a few spares for accidents.

What to do

Show the children the finished puppet that you have made, and explain that they can make one too if they wish. Give out photocopiable page 60 and talk about the names of the geometric shapes which form the puppet. Ask the children to colour the pieces of their clown, adding facial features, cut the shapes out and stick them together to make a figure. Show them how to mount the figure on one end of the lolly stick.

Next help them to assemble the box. This should be stuck onto cardboard before assembly, then a slit cut in the bottom to take the lower end of the lolly stick. The children may enjoy cutting pieces of patterned sticky-backed plastic to decorate the box.

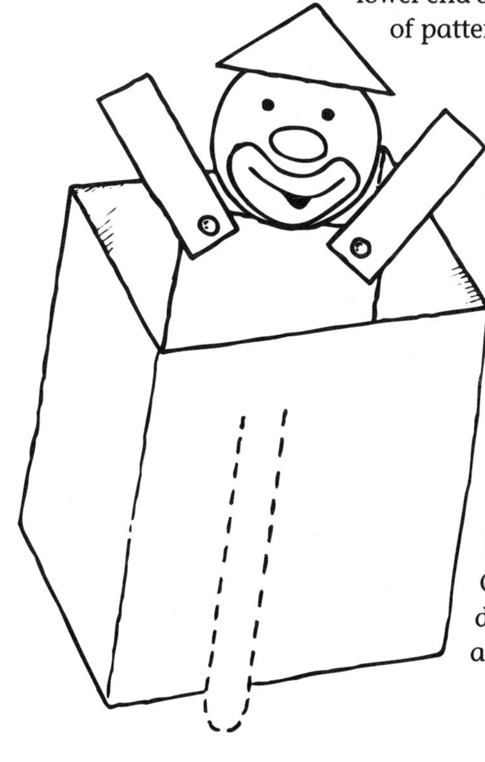

Questions to ask

What do we call this shape? Which part of the clown is this? Where are you going to stick that? What are you going to do next? What sort of face does the clown have? What can you make him do?

For younger children

Younger children could concentrate on assembling the figure, using a ready-made box such as a small cereal packet. They could also cover the box with sticky-backed plastic. Help them to make a slit in the bottom for their lolly stick.

For older children

Older children could try to design other figures using different geometric shapes for the head, body and arms.

Follow-up activities
- Build pictures using gummed paper cut into geometric shapes.
- Thread beads of different shapes to make patterns of two or three.
- Print in dough or Plasticine using geometrical shapes to make figures.

DOWN ON THE FARM

Learning objective
To develop sorting and counting skills.

Group size
Eight children.

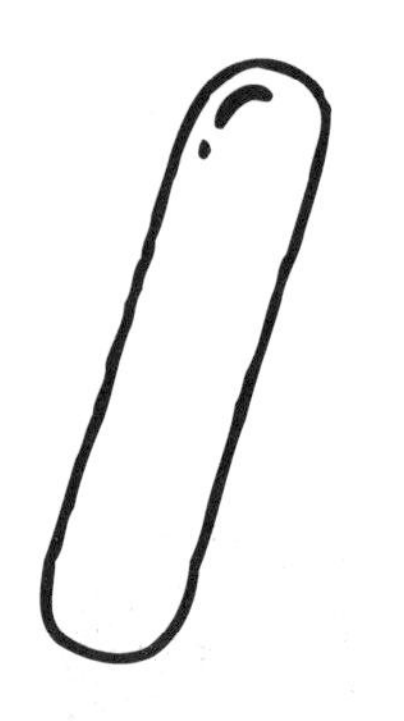

What you need

A visit to a farm/model farm/pictures of farm animals/photocopiable page 61 as a reference, green paper, paint, brushes, PVA adhesive, a thick marker, five sheets of paper, a modelling material such as terracotta clay, Newclay (air-drying), papier mâché or Mod Roc.

Setting up

Cut out rectangles of the green paper to act as fields. Make sure they are large enough for the animals you have. Select one horse, two sheep, three goats, four cows and five pigs (or any other animals in these amounts) and place these in a heap on the floor next to the fields. Take your group on a visit to a farm if you can, as this gives the activity more immediate significance for the child.

What to do

Sit on the floor with the children and ask them if they know the names of the animals. Invite them to sort each set of animals into their own field and to write the numbers in each set on a piece of paper and put it in the field too. Let the children choose a modelling material to make an animal of any kind, looking carefully at any models or pictures you have made available. Point out the features of each animal which make it different from the others – wool, udders, horns – and things which make it similar – number of legs, heads, tails and so on. When they have made their animals, leave to dry and then ask whether they want to paint them. Mix PVA adhesive with paint to give a shiny glazed effect. Once the models are finished, count how many of each animal there are and put them into sets.

Questions to ask

What did you see at the farm? What did you like best? Where shall we put the cows? What have you made? What does the clay feel like when you hold it? How are you going to make the legs?

For younger children

Younger children should use numbers one to three and only move onto higher numbers if they appear to understand (conserve) these. Give them any support necessary when they are making their animals.

For older children

Older children can use the same activity to explore numbers to ten, and could also, by looking at numbers of ears and feet, do some early investigation of multiplication.

Follow-up activities
- Using animal rubber stamps and a stamp pad, make sets of a given number.
- Make sets of animals with different colours of dough and animal biscuit cutters.
- Use photocopiable page 61 as a resource for farm counting and sorting activities. Ask the children to sort: things with four legs; with two legs; things with bricks; things with tails and so on.

Co-operation and sharing are readily developed when children are working on a creative activity together. In this chapter there are activities which will help children to understand other cultures, develop a sense of wonder and build their self-esteem.

COAT OF MANY COLOURS

Learning objective
To work together and learn to say 'Please' and 'Thank you'.

Group size
Four children.

What you need
The story of Joseph and his coat of many colours, such as *Ladybird Bible Stories*, a couple of children's coats (try jumble sales – make sure they are washed) in a dull colour, to be cut and glued, ribbons, beads, sequins, feathers, tinsel, strips of fabric, sweet papers, which could be used to decorate the coats colourfully, adhesive, scissors.

Setting up
Make sure the coats are large enough to fit the members of your group. Emphasise that we do not cut up our normal clothes, and remind them of this throughout the activity. CARE! Closely supervise them when they are handling small items like sequins.

What to do
Read the story of Joseph. Suggest that the group makes their own coat of many colours. Point out that they should say 'please' and 'thank you' when working together. Look at the materials you have provided to decorate the garment and talk about what you could do with them – stick or tie them on, cut holes and leave the lining showing through, stick sequins onto it. Encourage the children to make decisions about how they are going to decorate the coat. From time to time, ask them to stand back and look at the overall effect. Remember to say 'please' and 'thank you' to the children yourself. When the coat is finished, let each child model it.

Questions to ask
What shall we put on the coat? Where? How are you going to fix that on? What colours should we put here? How does that feel? What shall we do with the coat when it's finished?

For younger children
Younger children may refuse to join in, if they have been warned never to tear, dirty or cut clothes! Offer each child a piece of material to decorate, instead. These pieces could then be joined together to make a cloak.

For older children
Older children may be more fashion-conscious and enjoy re-styling more types of clothing. They will also enjoy designing on paper first, and making a list of the materials they intend to use.

Follow-up activities
- Have a week when you place great emphasis on saying 'please' and 'thank you' during the normal day.
- Write the words for the children, ask them to remember the spelling and put your writing away while they write it out.
- Put the coats or cloaks into the role-play area for free play.

FLOUR BATIK

Learning objective
To learn how to be confident and develop self-esteem by evaluating their own work.

Group size
Six children.

What you need
Examples of fabric dyed using the batik method, absorbent white cotton material (if bright colours are wanted – white synthetic fabric works but gives a pastel effect). Flour and water paste, food colouring (check for permanency), basins, fine brushes (size four or six), disposable plastic gloves.

Setting up
Cover all surfaces as this activity can be messy, and the food colouring can stain if spilled. Mix the flour and water to a creamy consistency with the children watching – this will make a coating on the fabric. Make a test-piece to see if it will block out the dye.

What to do
Show the children the pieces of batik fabric and explain how the blanking-out process works. Provide a 20cm square of fabric for each child, and invite them to paint a pattern onto the fabric using the flour and water mix. Once this has dried, they can then paint around their pattern with the food colouring and leave it to dry. Finally, they can put on plastic gloves and wash their batik fabric in water to dissolve the flour, leaving a white pattern on a coloured background. Call the children together on the carpet and ask them about what they did. Talk about what made them feel happy and what made them feel sad when they were doing the activity, and how they felt about the finished result.

Questions to ask
How did you make this pattern? Why did you choose this colour? What are you going to use it for? What worked well? How did you feel when that happened? What didn't work well? How did you feel then? What would you do next time?

For younger children
Younger children may find it difficult to paint with flour and water, so perhaps they would enjoy dripping the mixture onto the fabric in blobs and then blowing them with a straw. They could then do the rest of the activity, although they may not be able to suggest any changes for the future.

For older children
Older children could move on to tying string to make circular patterns, and perhaps using this on a T-shirt.

Follow-up activities
- Display the squares of batik either together like a quilt or separately, alongside professionally produced batik material.
- Draw a picture with a white wax candle then lightly paint over with a colour wash.
- At the end of any art activity, make a habit of asking the children what they liked and did not like. In this way, they will be constantly evaluating their own work.

LET'S MAKE A PATTERN!

Learning objective
To develop a sense of wonder.

Group size
Four children.

What you need

A set of marbling inks available from artist's suppliers – alternatively you could try mixing powder paint with a small amount of oil, this is not quite as effective but a lot cheaper – an eye-dropper, a shallow tray, tepid water, A4 paper, a spoon or stick to stir.

Setting up

Cover all surfaces, as water and paint slops everywhere. Pour the water into the tray.

What to do

Ask the children to carefully drop some of the ink onto the water using the eye-dropper. Restrict choices to two colours at first. Encourage the children to stir the water gently, to ensure that the pattern spreads over the entire surface. Talk about the pattern they have made, then suggest that they put a piece of paper onto the water, to see what happens. The pattern will transfer itself to the paper and leave the water clear. Let the children experiment with different amounts of colours, and different shapes and shades of paper, making sure that the marbled sheets are left to dry away from the water.

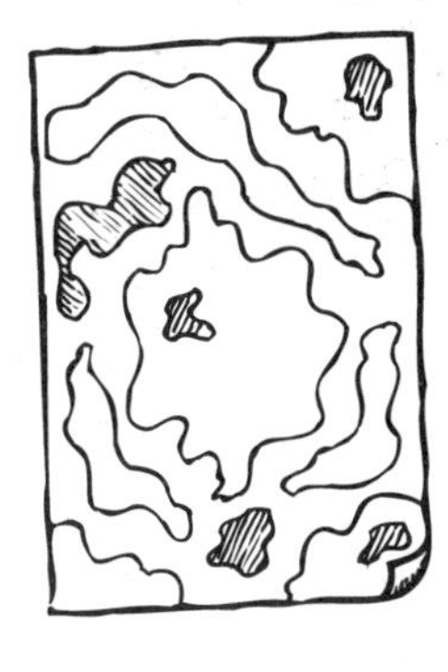

Questions to ask

What do you think will happen next? Why have you chosen those colours? What pattern have you made? What does it look like? What are you going to do with it? What could you use it for? How did you do that? What are you going to do now?

For younger children

Younger children will enjoy this activity, but might find it easier to use smaller sheets of paper, about postcard-size.

For older children

Older children could look at the end-papers and covers of old books which used marbling. They might then want to use their own sheets of marbling to decorate their own exercise books, drawers and so on.

Follow-up activities

- Look at some pieces of real marble and draw the patterns.
- Cut pieces of marbled paper and stick them onto another piece of paper marbled in a different colour.
- Use marbled paper to make realistic Easter eggs on Easter cards.

MEHNDI PATTERNS

Learning objective
To learn respect for people of other cultures and to respond to relevant cultural events.

Group size
Six children.

What you need
A piece of paper for each child, coloured felt-tipped pens (including a black one) or crayons, pictures of Mehndi patterns on the hands of Asian women or girls (alternatively you could draw some patterns on your own palms using brown felt-tipped pen instead of henna). There may be an Asian parent or teacher who could demonstrate how Mehndi patterns are applied with a stick.

Setting up
Draw around a child's hands in black felt-tipped pen. Photocopy this if you have access to a photocopier, otherwise draw around each child's hand in turn. CARE! At an appropriate time during the activity, explain to the children that they must not draw on their own hands.

What to do
Show the children the pictures of the decorated hands. Explain that during festivals and on special days, in India and Pakistan, women and girls decorate their hands and feet with intricate patterns. Point out some of the shapes used (see illustrations). Invite the children to design their version of these patterns on their outline hands. When the patterns have been completed to the children's satisfaction, they could be displayed on a large outline of a hand.

Questions to ask
Who puts patterns like this on their hands? Why? Which colours do you like best? What pattern are you going to make next? Where could we go wearing our Mehndi patterns? What do you want to do with your picture? Which pattern do you think is the best?

For younger children
Younger children could make hand prints of paint and then draw patterns onto them with felt-tipped pens when they are dry. They might also like to stick sequins onto the hand-patterns.

For older children
Let older children cut out their patterns, stick them into a book and write about them. They also might like to make Rangoli patterns at Divali.

Follow-up activities
- Put lengths of silken material for saris, chalwar and kameeze and other national dress into the role-play area to reflect our multicultural society.
- Celebrate different festivals during the year, including Eid, Divali, Chinese New Year and Hannukah.
- Draw around one child in your group on a piece of stiff card. Paint features, hands and feet and mount onto a sturdy support. Dress the figure in a different type of national clothing each week.

SELF-PORTRAITS

Learning objective
To build self-esteem, be sensitive to the feelings of others and learn to respect people of other cultures.

Group size
Six children.

What you need

Tissue-paper and gummed paper circles in various shades available from educational suppliers, sheets of coloured gummed paper, sheets of white paper. fine felt-tipped pens for eyes and lips, mirrors (plastic), paper, solid adhesive, wool or yarn in hair colours.

Setting up

Select the skin-shades of the tissue-paper circles and put them together in a pile. Put the rest away for another time.

What to do

Ask each child to look at the child next to her or (him) – be sensitive to individual children and encourage positive comment. Talk about the different colours of skin, from very pale to very dark. Compare the colour of children's eyes and the length, texture and colour of their hair. Then invite each child to stick a tissue-paper circle onto their sheet of white paper and draw eyes, nose, mouth and ears with the felt-tipped pens, sticking on hair if they want to. A half-circle of gummed paper will make the torso. This activity obviously has to be done supportively so that no child feels comparisons are being made in an unfavourable way, but that they are fine as they are.

This type of activity can highlight sensitive attitudes between people of different cultures. If this becomes a problem, develop a group handbook which can be sent home with the children, explaining your nursery/school's policy. Hopefully, this activity will emphasise that we are all different in some way.

Questions to ask

What is the same about your friend's face and your face? What is different? Why is this? What happens to our skin when we go out in the sun? What sort of hair have you got?

Follow-up activities
- Ensure that resources, especially home-made ones, reflect a wide range of ethnic origins.
- Provide books which have characters with different racial characteristics in positive roles, such as *But Martin* by June Counsel (Picture Corgi) and the series of books about Grace by Mary Hoffman (Frances Lincoln).

For younger children

Younger children could look at themselves in a full-length mirror and talk about how they look. They could then be invited to draw features on the tissue circle.

For older children

Older children could write a description of themselves: 'I have green eyes. I have auburn hair. My skin has freckles. Who am I?' Make a flap beneath their description to hide their name.

STARSTRUCK

Learning objective
To work co-operatively as part of a group.

Group size
Six children.

What you need

Circles and rectangles of paper, pearlised paint, plastic straws or sticks, gold, silver or coloured card, sequin strip, Cellophane, glitter, tinsel, feathers, metal foil paper, glitter gel, sequins/spangles, scissors, adhesive and spreaders, saucers or plastic palettes.

Setting up

Cut some of the card into strips about 20cms long and 2cms wide. Encourage the children to cut the card and the foil into approximate star-shapes. Put collage materials in saucers or palettes. Place all the materials on one table.

What to do

Invite the children to stand around the table and work together to create stars. Explain that there are lots of techniques they could use:

- by blobbing two or three different colours of shiny paint in the middle of the circle and scraping it in rays towards the edge of the circular paper;
- by cutting pieces of sequin strip, feathers and Cellophane and sticking them to the star-shaped card, then spreading adhesive and sprinkling glitter on top;
- by sticking the strips of silver card together like wheel spokes;
- by cutting holes in a star and sticking it on top of a different coloured card, so that the other colour shows through the holes, then sticking on glitter or spangles;
- any combination of the above or the children's own ideas.

Encourage the children to design their stars and work co-operatively together, interchanging materials as they see fit.

Questions to ask

What are you going to use to make your star? What do your friends need? How could you share? When can you see stars in the sky? How do you feel when you look at the stars? What are you going to do now? Why?

For younger children

Younger children should use just one of the techniques above initially, to give them plenty of time to thoroughly explore its possibilities, before introducing a different set of materials perhaps a week later.

For older children

Older children could design their stars, using thread-winding around a star-shape, weaving with paper strips, or printing with star-shaped potato-prints onto a larger star-shape.

Follow-up activities

- Display the stars with the words of 'Twinkle Twinkle Little Star', to develop early reading skills.
- Make a table display of different star-shapes, for example, Christmas baubles, candle-holders, biscuit cutters and so on. Press them into a lump of Plasticine or dough to make 'star' impressions.
- Bake star-shaped biscuits, ice and decorate them with jelly diamonds and silver balls.

WHICH DO YOU LIKE BEST?

Learning objective
To gain confidence by learning to make a choice.

Group size
Six children.

What you need

Assorted colours of dry powder paint, empty perforated spice tubs or old talcum powder containers, sheets of paper, icing sugar, a small amount of warm water.

Setting up

Together with your group, fill each of the empty shakers with the powder paint. Mix the icing sugar with a little water and spread a thin layer over the paper. Make enough for two sheets each.

What to do

While the paper is still damp, ask the children to sprinkle the powder paint lightly onto the paper surface and see what happens when it starts to spread. Let the children make two pictures and then decide which one they like the best. Accept the reasons the children give for their choices, and do not give your opinion of the relative merits of each picture, just agree with their choice.

Questions to ask

What colours are you going to use? What picture do you want to create? How did you do that? What is happening to the paint now? What does it look like? What would happen if the top came off your shaker? Which picture do you like the best?

For younger children

Younger children may find it difficult to decide if they like one picture more than another, so it might be better to ask them to choose which picture they want to take home.

For older children

Older children should be able to give detailed reasons why they have chosen one picture rather than another. They could then get together as a group and show their chosen pictures to each other, explaining why they chose them.

Follow-up activities

- Make choices throughout the day, such as: a snack, the dinner-menu, activities, books.
- Ice biscuits and drop different colours of food colouring onto them using an eye-dropper, then choose your favourite biscuit.
- Put some prints of famous paintings around the room. Each day someone chooses their favourite which is then put into a frame without glass and talked about at carpet-time.

MASKS

Learning objective
To study art from another culture and to show feelings in response to their experiences of the world.

Group size
Eight children.

What you need
Photographs or an actual example of an African mask, paper plates of 20cm diameter, elastic, felt-tipped pens, biros, pencil crayons, wax crayons, feathers, glitter, rice, artstraws, adhesive, scissors, food colouring or Brusho ink, paper towels, mirror (plastic).

Setting up
Colour the rice different colours by soaking it overnight in different shades of food colouring or Brusho ink. Dry on paper towels.

What to do
Show the children the photograph or the actual mask and ask them what they think about it. Tell them where it came from. Point out details which they may want to copy on their own mask in their own way. Look at the holes for the eyes and any other facial features. Let each child create their own design on a paper plate, using their choice of the collage materials. Help with attaching the elastic to the masks. Once they are completed, encourage the children to wear their masks and look at themselves in the mirror.

Questions to ask
How do you feel when you look at this mask? Who would wear a mask like this? What patterns can you see on the mask? What colours are on the mask? What have you stuck on your mask? Why? How are you going to make the mask fit you? What can you see in the mirror?

For younger children
Younger children could be given a paper plate with eye-holes already cut out, so that they can concentrate on the task of actually decorating their mask.

For older children
Older children might enjoy using needles and thread to sew patterns onto their masks.

Follow-up activities
- Try to make other types of masks, such as those used for masked balls on sticks, masks made from material, surgeon's masks and so on.
- Look at other African artefacts, such as textiles and sculpture. Make plain tunics using African-style fabric and place in the role-play area. Include strips of material to wrap around heads and waists.
- Introduce African instruments such as the 'talking' drum, and the cabasa. Use music from different countries as a stimulus to tidy away toys and get ready for a story.

KNOWLEDGE AND UNDERSTANDING OF THE WORLD

Young children want to know all about their environment, asking questions about how it works, and why things happen the way they do. In this way they form a mental picture of what our world is like, and this understanding provides a valuable foundation for future learning in history, geography, science and technology.

T-SHIRT DESIGN

Learning objective
To explore features of objects in the made world and to begin to understand the importance of design in clothing.

Group size
Eight children.

What you need
The book *Harry's Colours* by Jill Waterman (Burke), photocopiable page 62, coloured wool and yarn in the colours mentioned in the book, PVA adhesive in pots, spreaders, round-ended scissors, string or similar for a washing-line.

Setting up
Make a copy of photocopiable page 62 for each child.

What to do
Read the story with the children. It is about the colours of the clothes that a small boy (Harry) wears. Each page talks about a different item of clothing, with the name of its colour on the opposite page. Talk about the pictures as well as the print, asking the children to predict what will happen on the next page.

Let the children use wool and yarn to create a rainbow T-shirt for Harry, cutting pieces of wool to fit the width or length, and gluing them down onto their copy of photocopiable page 62.

Talk about the colours the children have chosen. Do they know their names? Cut out and hang up the T-shirt on a washing-line to make a display.

Questions to ask
What clothes do you like to wear? Why? What colours have you chosen for your T-shirt collage? How will you get that to stick? What are you going to do next? What would happen if your scissors wouldn't cut? What could you do?

For younger children
Younger children may not have the fine motor control necessary to cut strips of wool and then glue them down for the T-shirt. If however, you mount the T-shirt onto cardboard, they may be able to wind wool around it to make patterns, with some help in anchoring the ends.

For older children
Older children could design patterns on their T-shirt, or even write slogans. Using fabric-crayons and plain white T-shirts, they could have a fashion-show!

Follow-up activities
- Winding wool around cardboard shapes can make attractive hanging decorations for Christmas and Easter (bells, stars, eggs). Use a dab of adhesive to hold the loose ends in place.
- Read *Harry's Spots* and *Harry's Stripes*, also by Jill Waterman (Burke).
- Soak lengths of wool in shades of a colour of paint and place inside a piece of folded paper. Press down on the paper and pull the threads out slowly.

INSECT PLATES

Learning objective
To explore features of living things by observing the characteristics of insects, and to talk about their observations.

Group size
Eight children.

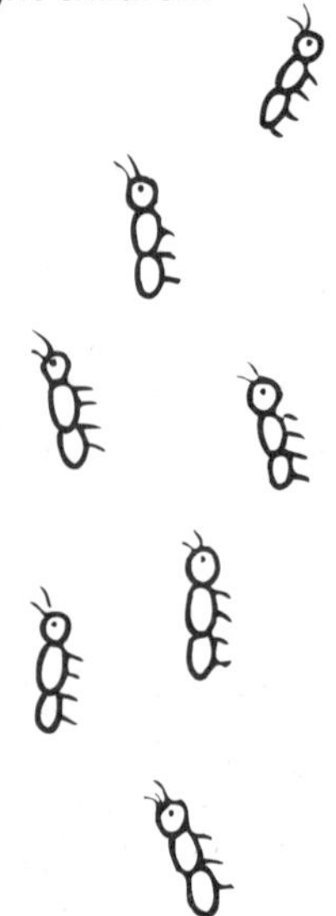

Follow-up activities
- Go on a hunt in the book corner for books with pictures of insects in them. Display them with the models.
- Play a 'beetle' game using Plasticine and pipe-cleaners. Have a dice with three blank faces and three faces with pictures of insect legs. The first lump of Plasticine with six legs wins.
- Put large plastic insects, available from joke-shops, in the water or the sand.

What you need
A plastic jar or some other transparent container in which to observe the insects safely, magnifying glasses (plastic), newspaper, cellular paste (without fungicide), paper plates, coloured paint, white paint.

Setting up
Mix the paste with water according to the instructions. Together with the children, tear up the paper and soak it in the paste. Once it has absorbed enough water, mix it so that it becomes mushy.

What to do
Go outside and collect insects with your group (be sensitive to children who are scared of some insects). Supervise this closely and emphasise the care needed when handling these living things. Show the children how to use plastic spoons or small brushes to gather the creatures into the plastic jars. Use the magnifier to look carefully at them. Discuss the number of legs and wings insects have, and the colours of their bodies. When you have finished observing them, discuss what you should do next. Prompt the children into suggesting that they take the insects back to where they found them.

Invite the children to make an insect shape by squeezing papier mâché onto paper plates to make an embossed effect. Keep referring to the characteristics of the insects. Put the plates on one side for a day to dry and then tell the children to paint the papier mâché white. Allow the white paint to dry for a day, and encourage them to paint their insect in the colours they find appropriate.

Questions to ask
What sort of insect is that? What is it doing? How does it feel on your hand? What looks different through the magnifying glass? What would happen if insects were as big as us? What colours has your insect got on it? What colours are you going to use to paint it?

For younger children
Younger children enjoy searching for and looking at insects, but might find several batches of appropriately coloured dough an easier medium for making their models.

For older children
Older children could try making large-scale papier-mâché or clay models, using chicken wire to reinforce the structure.

QUILLING

Learning objective
To begin to use a historical craft technique.

Group size
Four children.

What you need
Shallow cardboard shoe box lids, strips of stiff coloured paper 2cms wide and various lengths, a pencil for each child, adhesive, pictures or an example of quilling (quilling is the technique of rolling paper to make patterns which was very popular in Victorian times).

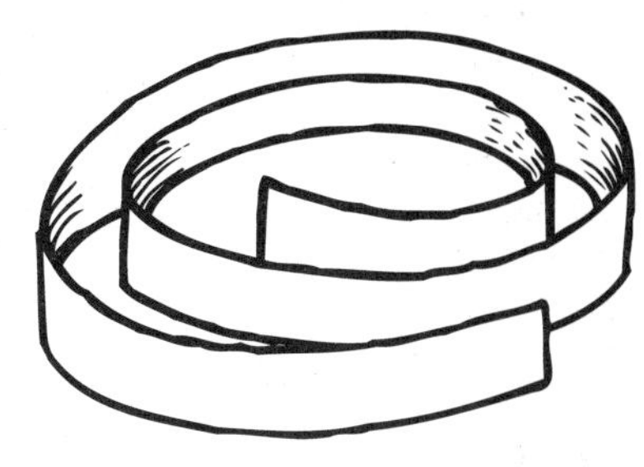

Setting up
The 2cm strips can be cut from A2 or A3 sized rainbow paper using a paper-cutter.

What to do
Look at the picture or example of quilling together. Talk about the history of quilling and the people who would have done it. Explain that quilling or rolled-paper work was popular in the eighteenth century, when ladies used to decorate objects with it. Tell the children that tea was very expensive in those days, and used to be kept in special, lockable boxes called caddies – King George III's daughter, Elizabeth, decorated a tea-caddy with elaborate quilling.

Demonstrate to the children how they can roll their strips of paper around their pencils to make curls or rings and then put them on their side into their cardboard shoe box lid 'frame'. Ask the children to make a picture and once they are happy with it, encourage them to glue the lower edges of their paper curls and stick them down.

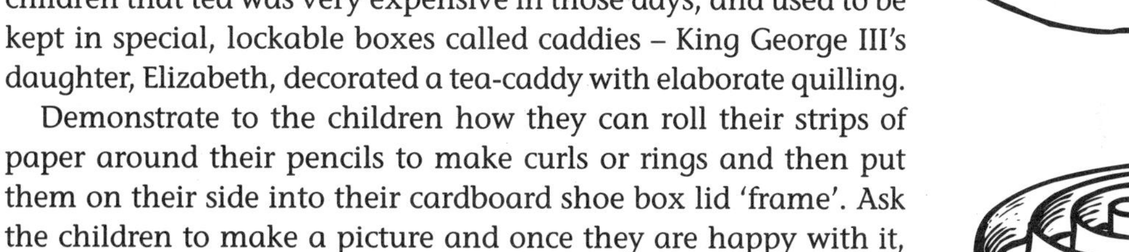

Questions to ask
What do you think of this pattern? Who do you think made it? How do you think they made it? How are you going to make your pattern? What colours are you going to use? How did you make that shape with the paper?

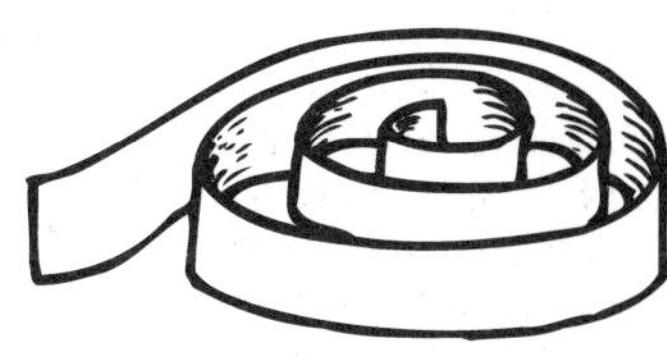

For younger children
For younger children, dispense with the frame and concentrate on rolling the strips of paper into curls and sticking them onto paper as, for example, Father Christmas's beard, the foliage of a Spring tree or just a pretty pattern.

For older children
Older children could try to use quilling to make a picture of a tree or a flower, using the blade of a blunt knife (closely supervised) to curl their paper.

Follow-up activities
- Make pictures of Christmas presents and decorate them with paper curls.
- Make hanging Christmas decorations by fastening bunches of curled paper together.
- Make curl patterns in pieces of potato, and then print with them.

A DARK, DARK PICTURE

Learning objective
To recognise events of the natural world and to investigate the similarities and differences of dark and light.

Group size
Eight children.

What you need
Grey or off-white paper, sticks of charcoal, white chalk, pencils, fixative or hairspray, and the following traditional story/poem:

In a dark, dark wood there was a dark, dark path,
And up the dark, dark path there was a dark, dark door,
And through the dark, dark door there was a dark, dark stair,
And up the dark, dark stair there was a dark, dark room,
And in the dark, dark room there was a dark, dark cupboard,
And in the dark, dark cupboard there was a dark, dark box,
And in the dark, dark box there was a GHOST!

Setting up
Find a place where you can sit with your group in the dark. Make sure those who are frightened of the dark are close to you.

What to do
In your dark place, say the poem to the children, clapping your hands when you get to the word 'ghost'. If you do not feel 'ghost' to be an appropriate word for your group, substitute another idea, or ask them what they think would be in the box. Repeat it, encouraging them to join in. Come out into the light and talk about the difference.

Now invite the children to make a dark, dark picture using the charcoal and the grey paper. When they have done this, ask them if they can make their picture lighter by adding white chalk. Talk the children through the technique of blending dark and light by rubbing with their fingers. When they have finished their picture, fix it for them by spraying with the hairspray. These pictures are effective mounted on silver paper.

Follow-up activities
- Use black, grey and white play dough to make a monochrome model.
- Colour the water in the water tray dark brown and add oatmeal and woodshavings to make a swamp. Put plastic dinosaurs in the swamp for imaginative play.
- Paint silver card with a mixture of black paint and PVA adhesive. When it has dried, use it as a scraper-board, making a silver picture on the black by scraping with cocktail sticks.

Questions to ask
How do you feel when it's dark? How do you feel when it's light? Which do you think is best? Why? What are you going to draw in your picture? What happens to your finger when you blend the charcoal and the chalk?

For younger children
Younger children who are frightened can just listen to the poem and join in, without going into a dark place.

For older children
Older children could try to shade objects to make them appear solid (3D) rather than flat, using charcoal for shading and chalk for the light sides.

PAINTING FLOWERS

Learning objective
To explore features of living things by observing flowers closely, and then making a 3D model.

Group size
Six children.

What you need

Several examples of interesting simply-shaped living flowers: single chrysanthemums, buttercups, cornflowers, poppies, containers to hold each variety – these could be plastic bottles with the tops cut off, salt dough made with flour, water and 20% salt, a wooden spoon to mix, magnifying lenses or a magnifying sheet (plastic), a variety of modelling tools to make patterns in the dough, paint in shades of appropriate colours, PVA adhesive, brushes of various sizes, an oven to bake the dough flowers.

Setting up

Mix your dough together with the children, talking about how it looks and feels at different stages.

What to do

Invite the children to look at the flowers. Encourage them to choose a flower, touch the petals and examine the way they are attached to the centre. Ask each child to talk to the others about the shape and number of petals on their chosen flower. Talk with the children while they make a flower like one of the real ones. Make a flower yourself and draw their attention to patterns made by features such as stamens and anthers. Bake the flowers, and the next day, once they have cooled, invite the children to paint them.

Questions to ask

Where could you find flowers like these? What grows in your garden? What have you made? How are you going to fix that onto your flower? Which flower do you like best? Why? How does the dough feel? How did you make that pattern? What colours are you going to use?

For younger children

Younger children should not be expected to produce a recognisable flower, but will enjoy manipulating the dough. You could introduce some pleasant scent into the dough, such as peppermint, lavender or banana, and ask the children to colour it an appropriate colour. (Make sure they aren't tempted to eat it.) The important thing for very young children is that they should have lots of different experiences and the opportunity to talk through them with a supportive adult.

For older children

Older children could mix colours on a palette, and then look at the flower of their choice and try to obtain the different shades.

Follow-up activities

- Make relief pictures of flowers using different colours of Plasticine on a flat board or a piece of card. If these are then painted with a mixture of half-water/half-PVA adhesive, the resulting glaze gives the effect of pottery.
- Make some edible biscuits in the same way, icing them using squeezy nozzles instead of painting them.
- Press the flowers to preserve them, then use them as part of a collage.

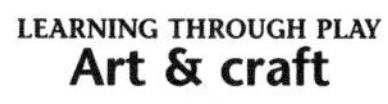

WOODEN SPOON PUPPETS

Learning objective
To explore and select materials when designing a simple puppet using a common household object.

Group size
Up to eight children.

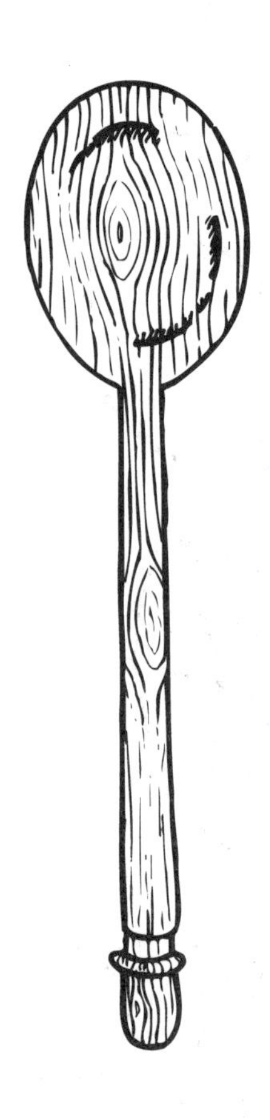

What you need

A wooden spoon for each child, a selection of pieces of fabric, Sellotape, (preferably in a dispenser), ribbon, string, scissors, adhesive, felt-tipped pens.

Setting up

Cut pieces of the material large enough to cover and wrap the handle of the spoon.

What to do

Look carefully together at the spoons and talk about what they are used for. Explain to the children that the spoons would make puppets if they had faces on the bowl and clothes on the handle. Show them all the materials, and ask them to decide how they are going to make a costume for their puppet, and to draw a suitable face on the bowl of the spoon. At Christmas time, the Nativity story makes a good focus for this activity, and each child can choose a character. At other times of the year, use well-known stories, such as the *Jolly Postman* by Allan Ahlberg (Heinemann), Maurice Sendak's *Where the Wild Things Are* (Picture Lions) or *Rama and Sita* by Ram Grovinder (Blackie).

One of the design problems the children will have to address is how to fasten the 'clothes' to the handle of the spoon so that they do not fall off. To do this they will need to cut lengths of ribbon or string, or use adhesive or Sellotape. They will also have to decide on which side of the bowl to draw the face.

Questions to ask

How did you stick that? What are you going to do next? What sort of puppet have you made? What can you do with it? What would your puppet say? What would it do in the story? How could you make it better?

For younger children

Younger children may find it enough to draw a face for their puppet. If they want to make clothes, but are finding it too difficult, you could show them how to make a hole in the middle of a piece of material, and glue it to the neck of the spoon to make a simple 'poncho'.

For older children

Older children who have had lots of experience with handling materials could be encouraged to include hair for their puppets, and perhaps design card arms over which the clothing could hang more realistically.

Follow-up activities
- Have a puppet-show using your wooden spoons.
- Look for other common household objects which could be easily made into puppets.
- Design string puppets using recycled materials.

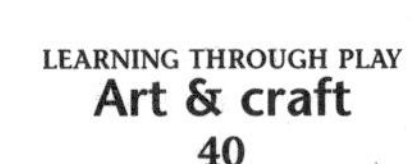

AUTUMN LEAF PICTURES

Learning objective
To explore some of the features of a natural object.

Group size
Six children.

What you need
Lots of autumn leaves, PVA adhesive, paper.

Setting up
Put the paper onto a table so that the children can rearrange the leaves before they stick them down.

What to do
Go outside with your group and find leaves of different autumnal shades. Bring them inside and sort them into sets of leaves of the same colour or shape. Discuss the appearance of the leaves, and how they feel to touch. Ask the children if they could make a picture using the leaves, arranging them first on their paper, and then gluing them when they are ready. Encourage the children to paint over their leaves with a PVA adhesive and water glaze. This will stop the leaves from drying out and will keep the autumn colours for longer. Display the children's pictures on an outline of a tree on the wall (see illustration).

Questions to ask
What do the leaves feel like? What sort of a noise do they make when you move them about? Where did we find these leaves? Do you like the colours? What is your picture about? What could you do next? Where are you going to put that leaf?

For younger children
Younger children should be invited to glue leaves which they have collected, inspected and sorted. They may not be able to see the possibilities for making representations of other objects, and this should not be expected of them.

For older children
Older children could co-operate and work on a group picture, designing it together, deciding on the shapes and colours and sharing out tasks and materials.

Follow-up activities
- Print with leaves, using different colours to represent the three 'leafy' seasons, for example: pinks, pale greens and yellows for spring, shades of dark and light green for summer.
- Punch holes in large thick leaves and experiment with lacing them together.
- Use leaves as stencils. Put a leaf on black paper and rub coloured chalk around its edges.

RAINY DAY PICTURES

Learning objective
To explore and talk about their observations of natural events by observing a feature of the weather.

Group size
Ten children.

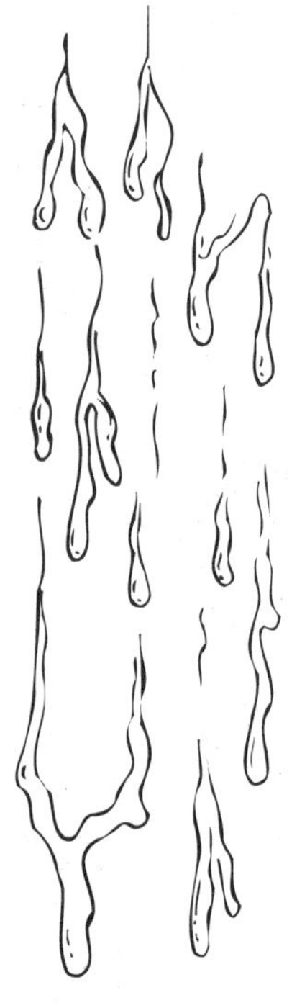

What you need
Sheets of paper, plastic straws or eye-droppers, Brusho ink in shades of blue, saucers, an easel (or if you don't have access to one, a board propped into a slanted position by a pile of books at the back), plastic tubs, water.

Setting up
Pour the ink into the tubs and saucers.

What to do
On a rainy day look at the raindrops on the windows. Point out to the children the way they zigzag from the top to the bottom. Show them how to use the eye-droppers or the straws to draw up their choice of blue ink and drip it onto the top of the paper on the easel/sloping board. Talk about what happens. Encourage the children to drip plain water on top of the ink, so that it runs down the page like raindrops and makes streaky patterns on the paper.

Questions to ask
How do you feel when it rains? What do you do? What do the raindrops look like? What happens when you drip the ink onto the paper? What sort of pattern have you made? What are you going to do next?

For younger children
Younger children could use paintbrushes and flick the ink and then water onto the sheet, if they have some difficulty controlling the straws or eye-droppers. Make sure this activity is controlled.

For older children
Older children could paint a picture and then treat it in this way to change it into a rainy day picture.

Follow-up activities
- Leave some paintings out in the rain for different lengths of time. Bring them in and look at them carefully. What has happened?
- Look at puddles. Stamp in them with wellingtons on. Make patterns in them using sticks and stones.
- Put a measuring jug or a plastic bottle outside and measure how much rain falls in a week.

PHYSICAL DEVELOPMENT

Cutting, tearing, folding and sticking all develop children's manipulative skills. Co-ordination of hand and eye plays a large part in the ability to write, while an awareness of spatial relationships is important for reading. In this chapter you will encounter action painting, bubble-printing and folding paper.

ACTION PAINTING

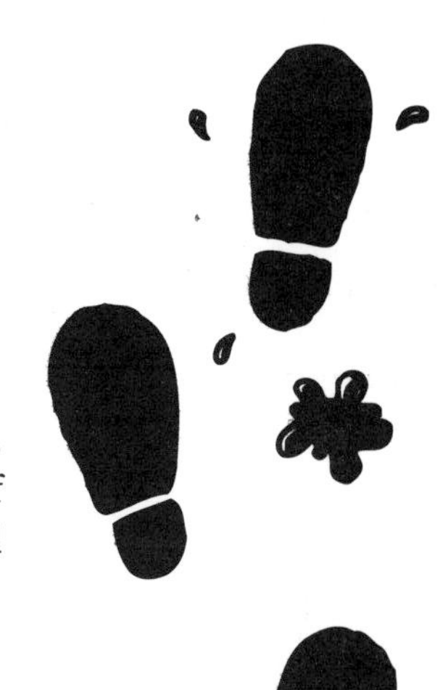

Learning objective
To move confidently and imaginatively with increasing control by developing large movements while painting.

Group size
Four children.

What you need
A fine day and some space outdoors where paint can be splashed, shoes from the role-play area, large sheets of paper, several sizes of decorators brush, a variety of colours of ready-mixed paint, several plastic trays or saucers, a scooter, a tricycle.

Setting up
Pour the paint into the trays. Put the paper on the ground outside.

What to do
Ask the children to choose a pair of shoes, put them on, stand in a tray of paint and then walk across the paper. When they have explored the tracks they can make, ask them to take off the shoes and suggest that they each find something with wheels. Paint the wheels with the big brushes and ride or push them across the paper. Examine the different patterns made this time. Finally, encourage the children to dip the brushes in the paint and flick paint over the tracks on the paper. Think of a name for their action painting.

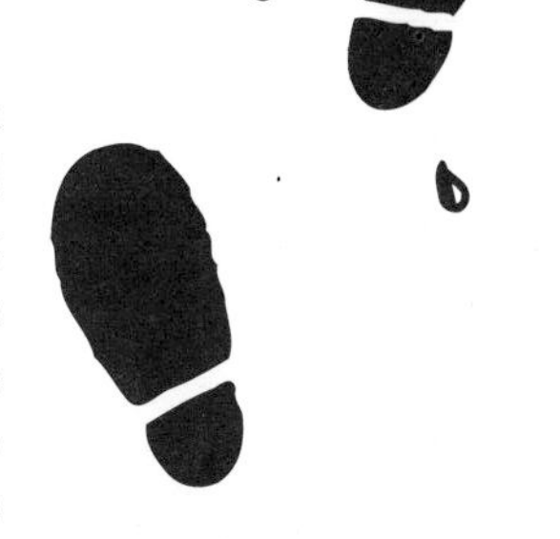

Questions to ask
What sort of footprints do you think these shoes will make? What has happened now? What else could you do? How could you find out what pattern this wheel will make? How could you make a different pattern? What are you going to do with that brush?

For younger children
Let younger children start by making patterns on the play surface on a hot day, using clean water and watching it evaporate. This could lead to making more permanent patterns using paint.

For older children
Older children could be asked to think of other tools which could be used to make paint-marks expressive of action, such as those used in sports like fishing, tennis, golf and so on.

Follow-up activities
- Stick some pictures of active figures onto cardboard and cut them out. Draw around one of these figures several times on a piece of paper and see how it creates the effect of movement.
- Use sponge or plastic rollers dipped in paint to create patterns reflecting arm movements.
- Use two colours of paint in squeezable bottles to make a dribbling pattern of lines.

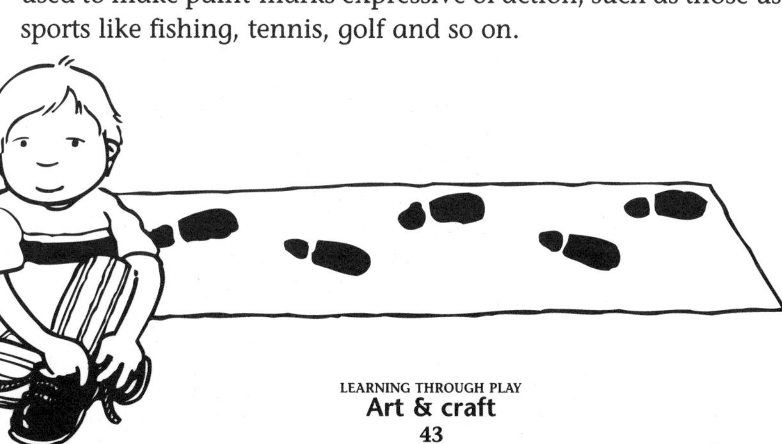

BUBBLING OVER

Learning objective
To make bubbles and use them for printing.

Group size
Six children.

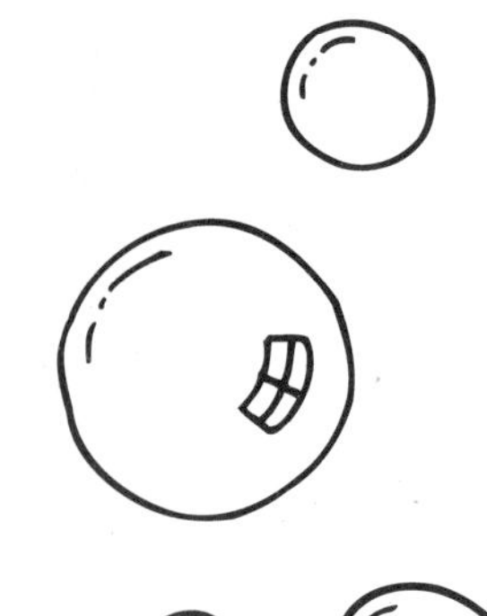

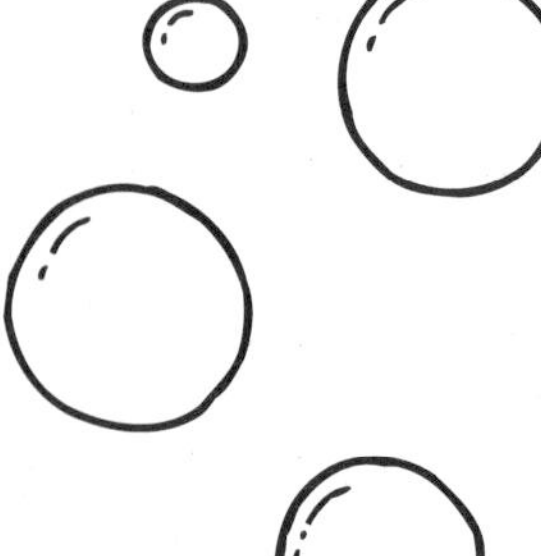

What you need
Bubble-blowing liquid and a bubble-maker, paper, different sizes and shapes of container such as an oval dish, a round dish, a square dish, a triangular dish, washing-up liquid, several colours of washable paint, plastic straws.

Setting up
Ensure the area where you will be working is well covered as bubble-printing can splash everywhere. Be aware of any allergies and if necessary limit contact with the washing-up liquid amongst affected children.

What to do
Blow bubbles for the children, and encourage them to have a go. Use the bubbles both indoors and out, especially if there is a strong breeze, since this will make the bubbles blow around madly.

Indoors, blow bubbles gently so that the children can observe them closely as they float. Encourage the children to talk about the swirling colours they can see, and the things that the bubbles do. Ask them to pour some paint and squeeze washing-up liquid into the shaped containers, blowing down the straw to make the mixture froth with bubbles. Tell them to place a piece of paper gently on top of the bubbles to obtain a print. Talk about the patterns made.

CARE! Ensure the children are carefully supervised and that they do not suck through the straws.

Questions to ask
What can you see in the bubbles? How do they make you feel? Where do you think this one will go? Does anyone use washing-up liquid at home? What for? What would happen if the bubble-maker was bigger? What shape is your picture? What happens to the bubbles?

For younger children
Younger children may find blowing down straws too difficult, so let them froth up the mixture with a whisk or the bubble-maker.

For older children
Older children could use different shaped bubble-makers made out of wire, and different colours of bubbles to compile a bubble-print picture, cutting shapes to size with scissors as well as trying to print them direct.

Follow-up activities
- Print with the ends of cotton-reels, cardboard tubes and pencils to make similar prints.
- Make a glitter snowstorm. Glue a small plastic figure to the inside of a screw top lid, put a spoonful of glitter in a plastic jar and fill with water. Screw the lid on tight and turn upside-down.
- Print using plastic bubble-wrap cut into shapes.

TABLE MATS

Learning objective
To develop simple, straight cutting skills.

Group size
Four children.

What you need

Scissors, A4 paper in rainbow colours, adhesive, glitter, spangles, sequins.

Setting up

If you have children who are left-handed, provide left-handed scissors for them to use. Make an example of a paper mat with a fringed edge, but without any patterns for the children to see. Make sure they are supervised when handling small items such as sequins.

What to do

Suggest that the children might like to make a present for their parents. Show them the mat and ask if they would like to make one and decorate it. Ask each of the children to make a pattern on your mat using the loose sequins or spangles, so that they can see what a finished mat would look like. Invite them to choose a colour from the rainbow paper. Ask the children to fringe both edges of their paper mats by making lots of straight cuts with their scissors. They can then decorate it to their satisfaction and take it home.

Questions to ask

Who are you going to give your mat to? Why? Which colour are you going to choose for your mat? How are you going to cut your paper? Which sequins/spangles do you think are the best? Why?

For younger children

Younger children find the act of cutting paper difficult to stop, once started, but should be encouraged to have a go and the largest ensuing piece of paper could be decorated as above.

For older children

Older children should be able to make cuts of equal length and more or less uniform width. Encourage them to produce more intricate patterns of sequins and so on.

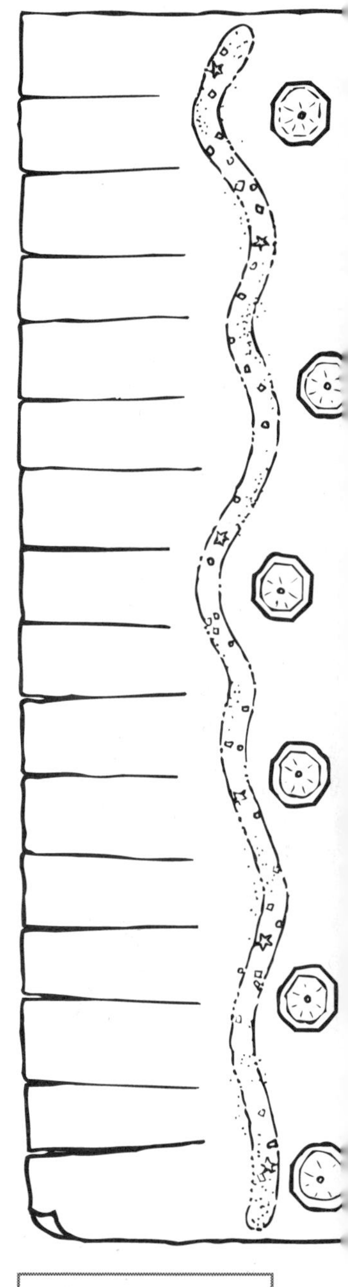

Follow-up activities

- Make some conifer trees by cutting green fringing for the foliage and winding it around a cone from the bottom up.
- Make fringing for native American costumes for the role-play area. Glue onto fabric with Copydex.
- Make a simple Christmas garland by twisting a long strip of fringed crêpe paper.

MOVING FIGURES

Learning objective
To move confidently and with increasing control and co-ordination by exploring different movements.

Group size
Four children.

What you need
A jointed artist's figure available from art suppliers, pastels and chalks, black paper, fixative or a can of cheap hairspray (for adult use only), a copy of the song 'Ready, stead, go' on the tape *Sticky Kids* available from Sticky Music.

Setting up
Make sure that your surface is covered, as pastels and chalks can produce large amounts of dust.

What to do
Sing the song with the children, and spend some time hopping, skipping, and walking around the room. Then introduce the wooden figure and encourage the children to explore what they can do with it, making it run, stand, gesture and so on. Ask them to arrange the figure in a posture that they want to draw. Point out the joints which help the figure move, then encourage the children to draw what they see using the chalks and pastels on the black paper. Once they have done this and are satisfied with their picture, you can 'fix' it (make it smudge-proof) for them using fixative or ordinary hairspray.

Questions to ask
What can you make your legs do? What can you make your arms do? Which do you like doing best – hopping or jumping? Why? What are you going to make the figure do? Which colour are you going to use to draw with? Where does the figure bend? Where can you bend?

For younger children
Let younger children enjoy the song and match the actions of the figure to the movements in the song, and then talk about them. They can experiment making marks with chalks and pastels, but should not be expected to produce a recognisable likeness of the figure.

For older children
Photocopy page 63 onto card and ask the older children to assemble a jointed puppet using split pins for the joints.

Follow-up activities
- Cut out figures from magazines or catalogues.
- Do some PE, moving in different ways to the sound of different percussion such as a tambourine, triangle and bells.
- Use bodies in different ways to make shadows against a screen or a wall. Guess what is being mimed.

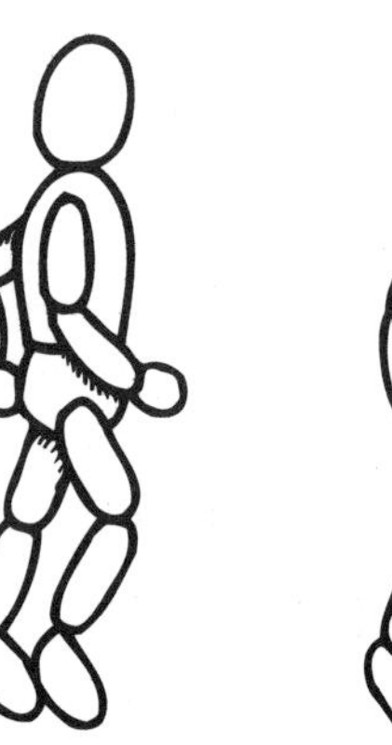

ELEPHANT TRUNKS

Learning objective
To fold paper.

Group size
Four children.

What you need

Thin grey or silver card, metallic paper the same colour, buttons, adhesive, a dinner plate (plastic), a book with pictures of African elephants in the wild.

Setting up

Together with the children, sort the buttons into pairs to use for eyes. Cut strips of card about 35cms long and 3cms wide.

What to do

Look at the pictures of the elephants and talk about their most distinctive feature – their trunk. Ask the children to make an elephant's head from the card using the dinner-plate as a template. Tell them to draw around the plate and then cut more or less on the line. The shape only needs to be approximate. Encourage the children to stick on the buttons for eyes. Show the children how to fold the strip of paper into a concertina and stick it between the button eyes. Displayed on a wall, they look great peering through jungle leaves (either made of crêpe paper or painted).

Questions to ask

Where could you expect to see elephants? What do they look like? What does an elephant use his trunk for? Which is bigger, a mouse or an elephant? How are you going to make your elephant? How did you do that? What are you doing now?

For younger children

Younger children might find the folding too difficult, so could concentrate on sticking a long trunk of thick wool onto their elephant face. If they cannot cut out the cardboard, help them or substitute with stiff paper.

For older children

Older children could search for information about elephants using reference books, and possibly visit the library. They could then make their own book about elephants, possibly in the shape of one.

Follow-up activities

- Make a fan or an aeroplane from pleated paper (fold over one end and staple to make the aeroplane's nose).
- Have a paper-folding table where folding can be experimented freely.
- Use a piece of concertina-folded paper as a body and stick a head, arms and legs onto it. The body can then be used for writing lists, menus, poems and so on.

DABBING

Learning objective
To develop manual dexterity.

Group size
Six children.

What you need

Sponges of different shapes and sizes, mixed powder colour or ready-mixed paint, a saucer for each colour of paint, paper.

Setting up

Cut a paper shape of whatever topic the children are working on at the time. It could be human figures, trees, leaves, shells, cars, houses, fish and so on.

What to do

Start by dipping fingers in paint and dabbing on the paper to make patterns. Once the children can do this, ask them if they can put their fingers together and dab. Move on to using the bottom of their fist, the heel of their hand, their knuckles and so on, to produce different shapes. This could take place over a week. Once the children are proficient at this, offer them the sponges of different shapes and sizes and ask them to dab a picture using any part of these, as they did with their hands.

Questions to ask

What other shapes can you make with your hand? How can you get that bit on the paper? What are you going to do next? What picture do you think you could make with this? What would happen if you used the side? What shape is that?

For younger children

Younger children need to spend a longer time using just the different aspects of their hands to make patterns. When using sponges, they are less likely to be able to see the relationships needed to make a picture, and may continue to produce repeating patterns. Let them try to develop a picture using their hands first.

For older children

Introduce stencils for older children. Create pictures which combine several individual stencils in the same way as stencils used for home decoration.

Follow-up activities

- Dab around the edge of a cut out shape to produce an image. Black paper and metallic paint is striking when used for this.
- Dab stencils onto windows at Christmas time, using paint mixed with washing-up liquid so that it sticks to the glass and comes off easily afterwards.
- Models made of recycled materials can be dabbed with sponges and paint mixed with PVA adhesive and sand to give a textured effect.

KITCHEN PATTERN PRINTS

Learning objective
To develop dexterity through printing with common household objects.

Group size
Up to eight children.

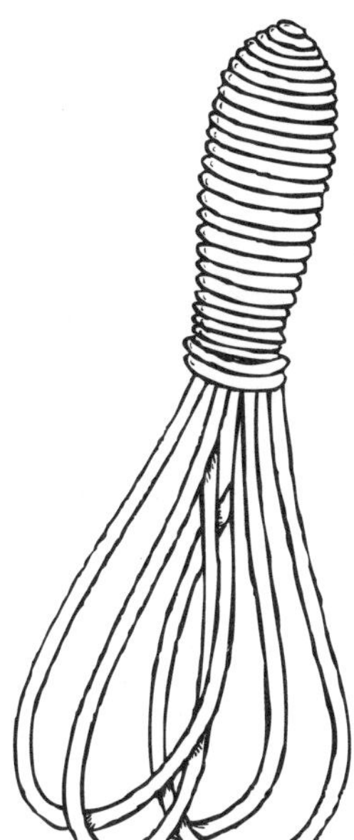
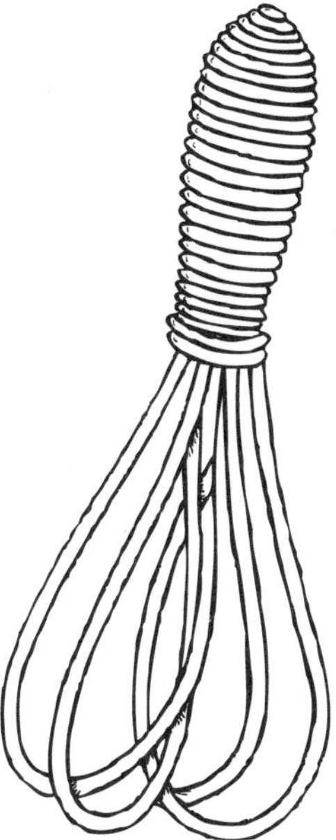

What you need

A selection of kitchen utensils which make a distinctive pattern, such as potato mashers, fish slices, crinkle-cutters, ladles, whisks and so on,food colouring, cellulose paste (without fungicide), a plastic bowl, several shallow dishes or trays, large sheets of paper.

Setting up

Test the implements you have to see if they print easily.

What to do

Together with the children, mix the paste according to the instructions, put into several shallow trays and add the different food colourings. The result should be of a thick 'dropping' consistency which can coat the implements for printing. Look carefully at the implements and talk about what they are used for at home. Encourage the children to choose an implement and print freely with it onto paper in their own choice of colours. Encourage them to print in several layers, so that the colours blend.

Questions to ask

What is that used for? What does the print look like? How did you do that? What are you going to do next? What sort of picture have you made? Which colours are your favourite? Which tool was the most fun to use? Why?

For younger children

Do not use metal tools with younger children, they should use safe plastic tools. If they would prefer, let them print and scratch the thick paste on the paper using their hands.

For older children

Older children who have had lots of experience with printing in various ways could use more elaborate shapes to print with, including plastic letters.

Follow-up activities

- Put the kitchen tools into the role-play area. Include a chef's hat and apron, together with bowls and pans.
- Use plastic knives and forks with play dough to practise cutting.
- Put washing-up liquid in the water-tray and use whisks to froth it up.

SNOWFLAKES

Learning objective
To handle appropriate tools safely and with increasing control by practising cutting.

Group size
Six children.

What you need
White paper, scissors with rounded ends, pencils, a tea plate to draw around, optional: a book showing enlargements of snowflakes and their unique shapes, sticky-backed plastic, string.

Setting up
Draw around the tea plate to make circles. Use several thicknesses of paper to make plenty of circles, as each child will probably want to make several snowflakes. If the children can do this themselves, so much the better. They should all have the chance to have a go.

What to do
This activity is best done on a snowy day! Look at the pictures of snowflakes if you have them. Show the children how to fold the paper circle into halves, then quarters, then eighths. Emphasise the importance of pressing the folds firmly. Demonstrate how to cut sections out of the paper without cutting all of the folded edge. Let them cut out whatever shapes they can and then unfold their snowflake to see what the effect is. The snowflakes could then be stuck onto circles of sticky-backed plastic and hung as mobiles from ceilings and windows.

Questions to ask
What is the weather like today? What did you do on the way here? What are you going to do when you go home? What can you make with snow? How does it make you feel? What happened when you cut that piece? What does it look like now?

For younger children
Younger children will need to have the circles cut for them. Let them fold the paper into quarters, and then cut off the three corners as a starting point.

For older children
Older children could cut elaborate patterns involving curls and spirals – these are a form of paper-sculpture which, when backed with black, silver or dark blue, display well.

Follow-up activities
- Fill some trays with snow and bring them indoors to play with. Provide small figures from DUPLO or Lego to encourage small-world play.
- Make some ice-cubes (or use snowballs and put them into two containers). Put one container outdoors and keep one inside – compare how they melt.
- Place small attractive objects into freezer trays and pour water over them. When frozen, place them into a water tray so that they will melt slowly and discover the treasure inside.

For young children to express their feelings and ideas in creative ways and to develop their imagination, they need plenty of opportunities to explore what they hear, see, smell, and touch. In this chapter you will find activities which look at famous artists, explore textured paint and look at moods in music.

FEATHERY FRAMES

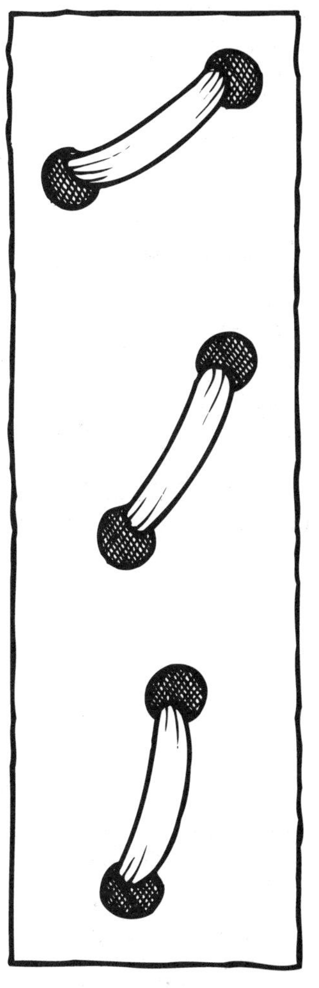

Learning objective
To create a unique frame for a photo or a painting.

Group size
Four children.

What you need

Sheets of brightly coloured A4 card, fairly stiff to stand up to children's handling, a single hole punch, rolls of the thin ribbon used for gift-wrapping, sequins, coloured collage feathers, large-eyed plastic craft needles, adhesive, sticky tape, pictures or photographs.

Setting up

Make sure each child's name is on their sheet of card. Ensure that the pictures or photos to be framed leave at least a 5cm margin.

What to do

Make holes at random in the 5cm margin frame of the card. Show the children how to thread the plastic needles with the ribbon. Use sticky-tape to fasten one end of the ribbon to the frame and encourage the children to 'sew' with the ribbon, in and out of the punched holes. Wrapping the thread around the frame, only adds to the charm of the finished frame.

Fasten the end of the thread to the back of the frame. The children should then choose three feathers and four sequins which they can thread through their sewing and stick on to their frame. Two holes punched at the top of the frame and a small piece of ribbon threaded through will make a hanger.

Questions to ask

What colour feathers have you chosen? Where are you going to put them? Why? What are you going to do with this picture when it is finished?

For younger children

Miss out the sewing and just let them stick scraps of ribbon onto the frame with their feathers and sequins.

For older children

Older children could attempt to sew a pattern of overlapping stitches around the edge of their frame.

Follow-up activities

- Make your own sewing cards by laminating pictures from magazines and punching holes in them. Use laces with reinforced ends for threading.
- Use some strips of hessian to weave strips of cloth, paper and net to make an interesting surface.
- Punch holes on pieces of cloth and sew with string, raffia or wool. Then join them together to make a wall-hanging.

HERE IS A BOX

Learning objective
To explore sounds and develop imagination.

Group size
Six children.

What you need

The poem 'Here is a box' (source unknown).
Here is a box, (hold out fist)
put on the lid (place other hand flat on the top)
I wonder what inside is hid? (lift lid)
Oooh! It's a (make a sound effect) *without any doubt.*
Open the box and let it out!
A choice of drawing tools such as felt-tipped pens, crayons, coloured pencils, paper for drawing.

Setting up

Make sure crayons and coloured pencils have been sharpened.

What to do

Decide what to have in the 'box': farm or zoo animals, everyday objects such as a telephone, an ambulance or fire-engine and so on. Say the poem with the children using the relevant sound effects. Repeat the poem this time encouraging them to suggest noises which could come from the box, as well as guessing what is in it. Ask them to each draw a picture to show what they would like to find in the box.

Questions to ask

What's in the box? What sounds can you make? What are you going to put in the box? What sort of noise does it make? What do you like to do? How could that go in the box? What would you feel if you were in a box?

For younger children

Young children will enjoy saying the poem and guessing the sounds. They will probably be able to suggest other sounds and objects, but may need some help in choosing what to draw.

For older children

Older children enjoy revisiting this poem when they have experienced it as younger children. Ask them to think of describing words for the thing in the box: 'a great golden lion', 'a long leggy giraffe'. Can they describe how it comes out? Does it, slink, slide, slither, leap or trot?

Follow-up activities
- Using an outline or 'net' of a box, make some boxes to decorate, or else use recycled boxes. Decorate them with shells, seeds, pasta and so on, then spray them with gold or silver paint.
- Find a very large box to climb into – then decide what you are in the box, and how to get out!
- Gift wrap some empty boxes of different shapes and sizes. Leave them in the role-play area for imaginative play.

TEXTURED PAINT

Learning objective
To explore texture and respond to what they touch.

Group size
Eight children.

What you need

Ready-mixed or powder paint in black, white and one other colour (for example, blue for a sea theme, orange for Autumn), five pots to hold the different shades of paint, PVA adhesive, spatulas, sticks and scrapers, a choice of black or white paper, silver sand, glitter, white washing powder, sawdust.

Setting up

Together with the children, mix five shades of your chosen colour. Your original colour can be one shade. Mix one pot with mostly white paint and a hint of colour and another pot with half black paint. Mix two more with about one quarter white paint and one quarter black paint to give you five shades. To each pot add one of the materials mentioned above. Cut the paper into 'themed' shapes, for example: for autumn you might have leaf-shaped paper, for a sea theme fish-shaped paper.

What to do

Invite the children to spread the textured paint over their chosen paper. Encourage them to feel the paint with their fingers, describe how it feels, and to paint with their fingers if they wish. When the paint is dry, feel the paint again and talk about how it feels now. Use descriptive touch language – smooth, silky, scratchy, lumpy, grainy, rough, hard, soft.

Questions to ask

What paint are you going to choose first? What is in it? What can you feel when you touch it? What sort of pattern does it make? Why have you picked that scraper? How are you going to spread the paint? Why does it feel different now?

For younger children

Younger children might benefit from being introduced to just one texture at a time and exploring all its possibilities before being offered a range of textures.

For older children

Older children could create their own textured paints and produce pictures with a sculptured effect, using all sorts of seeds such as rice, poppy-seeds, lentils and so on to make rough waves, crusty snow or waving corn.

Follow-up activities
- Put some jelly into a water-tray and experience this texture.
- Put some old stockings into the dry sand and fill them – then feel the slippery texture.

TAKE A PICTURE

Learning objective
To develop an increasing ability to use their imagination and observe through a painting by a famous artist.

Group size
Eight children.

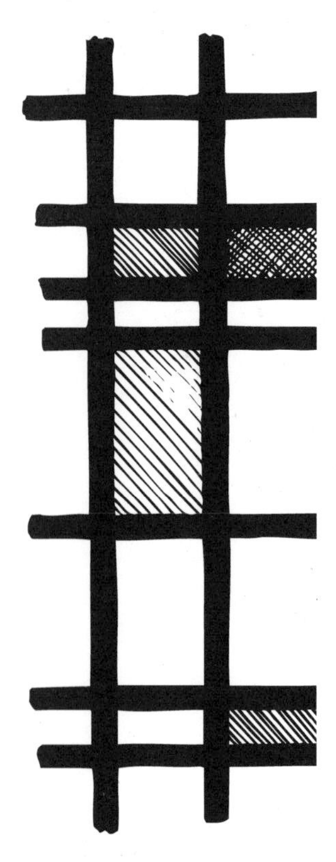

What you need
A copy of an abstract painting of rectangles by Piet Mondrian, such as *Composition with red, black, blue, yellow and grey*, black sugar paper, gummed paper in a range of colours including white, scissors, saucers, sponges, water.

Setting up
Put some water in the saucers and place the sponges in it. This will act as a dampening medium – much more hygienic than licking the paper. Cut out blocks of the gummed paper.

What to do
Look at the picture carefully. Talk to the children about where the artist has placed his blocks of colour, their size and their shape. Ask the children if they would like to make a picture like the print they have been looking at. Invite them to place blocks of coloured gummed paper on their paper, leaving an edge of black all the way round. When the children have composed the pictures to their own satisfaction, encourage them to stick their shapes onto the paper, using the sponges to wet the paper. Display the pictures together with the Mondrian print that inspired them.

Questions to ask
What do you think of this picture? What different shapes can you see? What do you feel when you look at it? What does it remind you of? How are you going to make that stick? Why have you put that colour there? What are you going to do next?

For younger children
If the children are having difficulty composing a picture, encourage them to place the shapes anywhere on their paper and accept any reasons they give.

For older children
Older children may be able to cut out the shapes themselves.

Follow-up activities
- Use slabs of Plasticine to make a Mondrian picture, cutting the edges with a knife.
- Print on black fabric with paint and PVA adhesive using various sized rectangular shapes such as plastic bricks.
- Change the shapes into circles or triangles. Is the effect the same?

TILES

Learning objective
To experience and respond to some of the characteristics of clay. To use a wide range of tools to express ideas.

Group size
Four children.

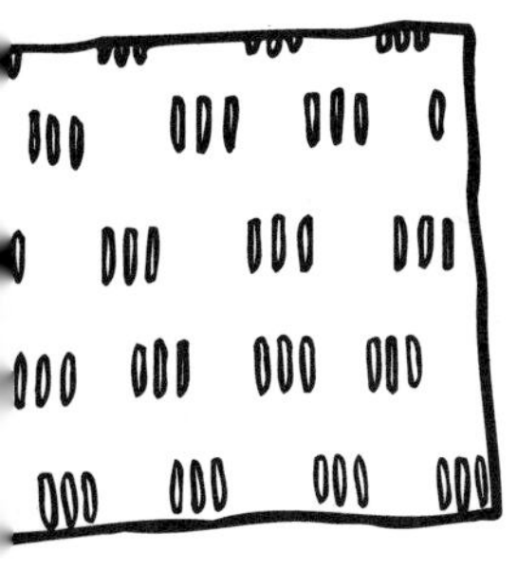

What you need

Newclay or some other self-drying modelling material, rolling pins, mark-making tools such as plastic scrapers, combs, cocktail sticks, blunt knives, forks and so on, any other tools which could shape clay such as a pasta-machine, a garlic press, a latticed potato masher, examples or pictures of patterned tiles, saucers or bowls, water, tea towels, a tile to use as a template.

Setting up

Put the water in the bowls and dampen the tea towels. Put them on the clay from time to time so that it is kept damp and malleable until the work is finished. Before starting this activity the children should have had plenty of opportunities to explore the texture and qualities of clay in free-play situations. They need to have pounded, squashed, poked, pinched and rolled the clay with a large variety of tools before attempting to make a tile.

What to do

Show the children the example of a tile which you have obtained. Can they see what has been done to the tile to make the pattern? Demonstrate the different patterns they could make on their tiles using the equipment you have provided. The garlic press is particularly fascinating as the fine filaments ooze out onto the tile and can look like hair or grass. Show the children how to roll the clay and cut around a template to make a basic tile, then invite them to decorate it as they see fit. Put the finished tiles somewhere safe to dry.

Questions to ask

What does the clay feel like when it is wet? What happens if you add lots of water? What can you do with the clay? How did you make that pattern? What pattern do you want to make now? What tools will you need?

For younger children

Some younger children will not be able to cut a tile from a template without adult help, but all children should enjoy making marks on their tiles.

For older children

Older children could extend their experience from Newclay to potting clay, and if there is a kiln available, these tiles could be fired to biscuit stage and then painted with glazes and fired again.

Follow-up activities

- Make mud-pies using soil-based potting compost and water in the sand tray.
- Use Plasticine glued to card as a base for a tile and decorate with beads and seeds. Brush over with PVA adhesive for a glazed effect.
- Press clay onto objects with a patterned surface and look at the back-to-front effect this creates.

ROCK ON!

Learning objective
To explore texture, shape and form in three dimensions by creating a 3D sculpture using pebbles.

Group size
Eight children.

What you need
Eight smooth pebbles, wool, string, paint, PVA adhesive, brushes.

Setting up
Mix some PVA adhesive with the paint so that it will stick to the pebbles.

What to do
Look at and feel the stones. Pass them from hand to hand. Talk about their texture and colour, where they have come from and so on. Ask the children if they would like to paint a stone, or decorate it by wrapping string or wool around it, or both. Then encourage the children to decorate their stones how they like, painting under or on top of the wool.

Questions to ask
What does your stone feel like? What does it look like? What colours are you going to use on your stone? Why? How are you going to fasten the end of your wool? What would happen if you dropped your stone?

For younger children
Younger children should concentrate on painting their stone, as winding the wool around it may be beyond their manual dexterity skills.

For older children
Older children could make patterns with the wool, sticking it down with adhesive and then painting if they wished. They could also include textures using sand or seeds in the paint.

Follow-up activities
- Make a collection of natural 'found' objects and decorate them.
- Cover a stone with Plaster of Paris and use fingers or tools to scrape patterns in the plaster. Press small objects such as pasta shapes into it, and finally spray or paint it.
- Paint small pebbles to look like insects or animals. Stick on paws or legs cut from card.

MUSICAL MATCHING

Learning objective
To listen, recognise and respond to different moods in music.

Group size
Six children.

What you need
A cassette of short (one or two minutes) excerpts of music of at least three different kinds which are suitable for each of the three bears – examples could be Wagner's *Ride of the Valkyrie*, a Brass Band playing 'Coming home' and Tchaikovsky's *The Dance of the Sugar Plum Fairy,* three soft teddy bear toys, a cassette player, felt-tipped pens, scissors, photocopiable page 64.

Setting up
Ensure that the children know how to switch the cassette on and off.

What to do
Show the children the three toy bears and talk about them. Ask the children what they think of when they see each bear. Talk about the sort of noises the children would expect from each of the bears. Play the tape and tell the children to listen carefully to the different kinds of music. Ask them which piece of music in their opinion goes with each bear. Invite them to choose one of the finger-puppets (page 64), colour and cut it out, then make their finger-puppet dance to the music they have chosen.

Questions to ask
What sort of voice would Baby Bear have? Mummy Bear? Daddy Bear? What sounds would go with each one? Which piece of music makes you think of Baby Bear's voice? Mummy Bear's? Daddy Bear's?

For younger children
Younger children may not match the toys to the music you expect. Just ask them to choose music for Baby Bear after listening to all three pieces of music. Accept what they offer and talk with them about their choice.

For older children
Older children could try to make appropriate music for the three bears using simple percussion such as chime bars, drums and maracas.

Follow-up activities
- While playing a piece of music, paint a picture, moving your brush in time to the music.
- Use music as a stimulus for gathering on the carpet or tidying away toys.
- Make headphones and a cassette player available so that children can choose to listen to different types of music each week. Both pop and classical compositions are suitable.

MAKING YOUR MARK

Learning objective
To explore a range of mark-making materials and to use tools to express ideas and communicate feelings.

Group size
Eight children.

What you need
The book *Red is Best* by Kathy Stimson (OUP), paint in the three primary colours (red, blue, yellow), tools to use with the paint – lolly sticks, twigs, toothbrushes, plastic straws, spoons, pencils, a table with a protected surface, paper to paint on (old newspaper is fine).

Setting up
Put the paint pots, paper and tools on the table.

What to do
Read the story *Red is Best* with your group. This story concerns a little girl who feels happiest when she wears her red socks, scarf, tights and dress. It describes how her red socks make her feet want to dance.

Talk about what the child felt when she wore her red clothes. Then invite the children to paint a picture using just one colour they like best. Before starting, ask the children to write their name on the paper. Talk about the shape of the letters in their name.

Whatever marks the children make, praise their efforts and ask them to read or describe what they are to you. Encourage the children to use all the different tools you have provided to make different types of marks on the paper.

Questions to ask
What is your favourite colour? How does it make you feel? What have you got that is that colour? What do you use it for? What sort of a mark have you made? What would happen if you used the other end?

For younger children
Younger children love to have the opportunity of feeling paint on their hands. Let them feel one colour of paint and then finger-paint on a plastic surface as well as paper. Spooning the paint up and letting it dribble back into the tray or onto paper is also a satisfying activity for younger children.

For older children
Older children could organise their own resources, deciding what they want to do, and collecting the tools and equipment they need. They could also mix shades of their chosen colour and find describing words for the colours they have made, such as 'glistening, cool, jungly' (for different shades of green).

Follow-up activities
- Read some poems about colours such as the ones found in *Out of the Blue* by Hiawyn Oram (Picture Lions).
- Dye some hollow pasta shapes with different strengths of food colouring and make necklaces with the different shades.
- Change the colour of recycled materials so that they 'belong' to the colour table – put out a single colour of paint, chalk and felt-tipped pen.

PHOTOCOPIABLES

PHOTOCOPIABLES

Name ______________________________

Name ________________________________

Name ___________________________

Name ___________________________

Name ________________________________

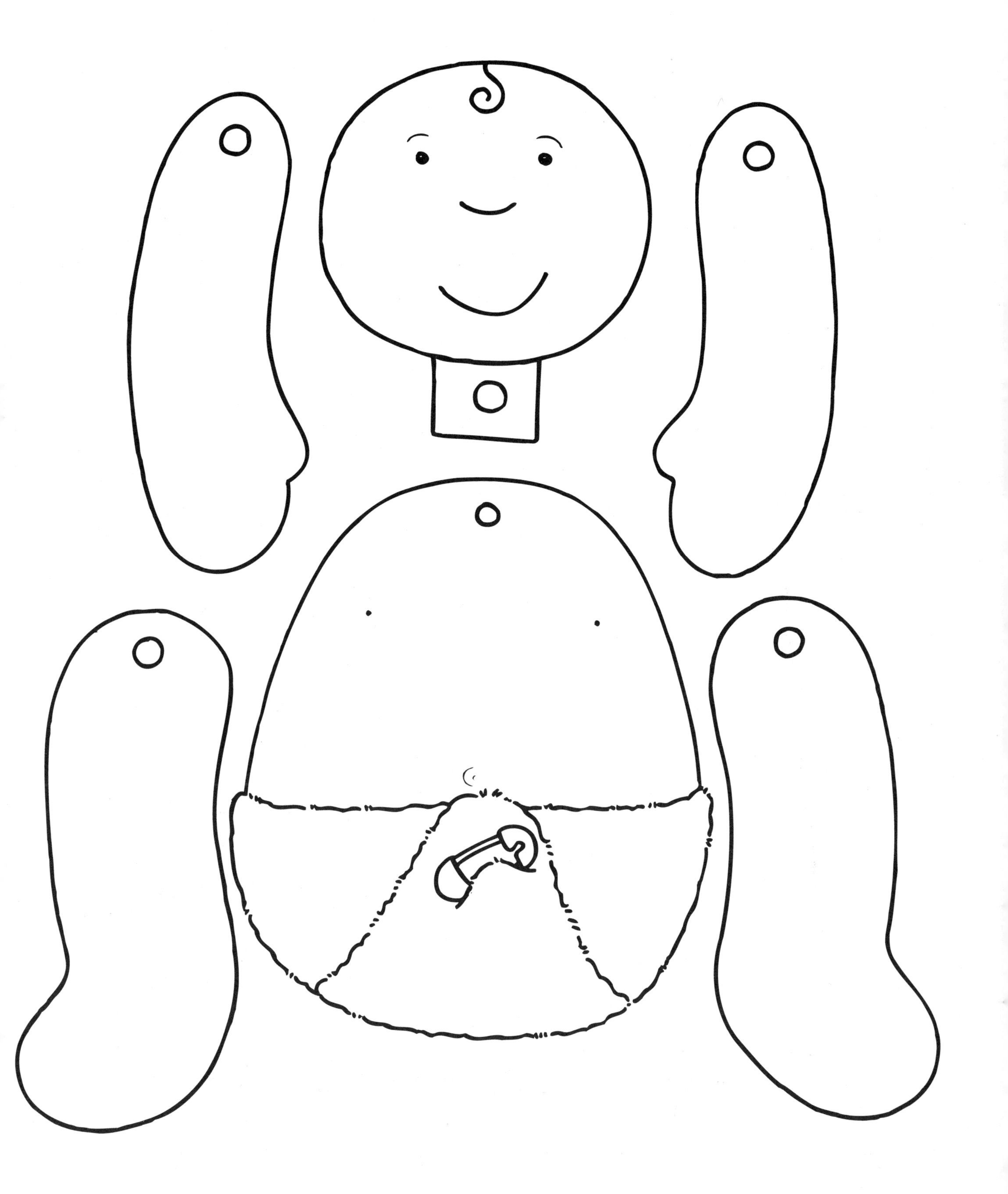

Name ______________________________